"WHO WOULD HAVE
DREAMED AT THE
BEGINNING OF THE
SEASON THAT THIS
TEAM – OR ANY TEAM
– WOULD WIN
116 BALLGAMES?
IT'S ALMOST
INCOMPREHENSIBLE."
– Manager
Lou Piniella

MARINERS 2001

A JOY RIDE INTO THE RECORD BOOKS

BY THE SEATTLE POST-INTELLIGENCER

Featuring writers David Andriesen, John Hickey, John Levesque, Art Thiel and
Laura Vecsey, and photographers Dan DeLong, Paul Kitagaki Jr. and Mike Urban.

Seattle Post-Intelligencer

MARINERS 2001:
A JOY RIDE INTO THE RECORD BOOKS

Publisher: Roger Oglesby

Editor: Glenn Drosendahl

Designer: Mark Evans

Text editor: Nick Rousso

Photography editor: Don Marquis

Graphics editor: Celeste Bernard

Contributing writers: David Andriesen,
Holly Cain, John Hickey, John Levesque,
Ted Miller, Jim Moore, Dan Raley, Art Thiel,
Ronald Tillery, Laura Vecsey

Contributing photographers: Gilbert W. Arias,
Renee C. Beyer, Dan DeLong, Grant M. Haller,
Paul Kitagaki Jr., Meryl Schenker, Mike Urban

Consulting editors: Lee Rozen, Pete Wevurski,
Ron Matthews, Neal Pattison

Other contributors: Jim Woolace, Mike Mahoney

Distributor: Sasquatch Books, Seattle

Printer: Graphic Arts Center, Portland, Oregon

Cover photograph by Dan DeLong

Title page photograph by Dan DeLong

Contents page photograph by Grant M. Haller

Pages 8 and 63 photographs by Mike Urban

Section front photographs by
Paul Kitagaki Jr. (pages 9, 31 and 73)
and Dan DeLong (pages 17, 51 and 79)

For information, see www.seattlepi.com, or write:
Publisher, Seattle Post-Intelligencer,
P.O. Box 1909, Seattle WA 98111-1909
For bulk sales, contact Sasquatch Books, (800) 775-0817

ISBN 0-9624559-8-9

TEAMWORK
These Mariners showed us 116 ways to win

FROM MODEST EXPECTATIONS came big results. The Seattle Mariners, who were widely picked to finish second or lower in their division, won more games than any team since 1906. It was one of the best seasons in baseball's long history.

The Mariners already had legions of fans, but few could have seen this coming. The sheer success of it would have provided plenty of material for a book, but that wasn't our only reason for doing this one. We also were motivated by how the Mariners did it – with remarkable teamwork – and when they did it – at a time when our city and nation truly needed a lift.

The September 11 terrorist attacks on New York and Washington, D.C., killed thousands and left us wondering what was next and if we would ever again feel safe. These events reestablished priorities. They reminded us that family and friends come first, that real life is more precious than we ordinarily think, that sports are only entertainment.

Or are they? The Mariners were part of our healing process. After a week of national mourning, baseball returned to Safeco Field in a way that was both touching and unifying. A community of nearly 50,000 at the ballpark and millions more

through the media shared a moment of reflection and renewal. And when the Mariners clinched the American League West championship the next night, they marked the occasion with appropriate restraint and dignity. The sight of Mark McLemore carrying the U.S. flag and of players kneeling, their heads bowed in prayer, will stay with this city for a long time.

The Mariners came through that night. By then, we knew they would. This was more than a good team. It was a special group of people, doing their jobs with grace and humility and, in happier times, joy that was contagious.

Winning 116 games gave us plenty to celebrate. How the Mariners won them is a source of collective pride and a lesson in how to do good work. Together.

This book features in words and photographs the best of the P-I's Mariners coverage – not only the wins and losses, but also the qualities that made a special team. It chronicles a season the likes of which none of us may ever see again. We at the Post-Intelligencer hope you enjoy it.

– Roger Oglesby,
Editor and Publisher

CONTENTS

THE CHALLENGE

MAKING HISTORY

No superstars? No problem for this fun-to-watch team

By John Levesque

INCREDIBLE. PREPOSTEROUS. ABSURD.

Pick a word to describe the Seattle Mariners' 2001 season and it could just as easily apply to the way it ended.

Mariners broadcaster Rick Rizzs described it as a team with more records than an oldies radio station. Emphasis on TEAM.

But for a franchise that won 116 regular-season games and set dozens of other team and individual records, what seemed at one time an entitlement became an unreachable star in the hostile firmament of the postseason.

Believe it or not, that's OK. There are other words to describe the 2001 Mariners season that will resonate longer in the hearts of all but the most cynical.

Exhilarating, for one.

Fabulous.

And – after the sour taste of October has had time to dissipate – absolutely delightful.

Besides, the noted clubhouse philosopher Plato once said: "The beginning is the most important part of the work."

And what a beginning it was. After winning 20 of 25 games in April, the Mariners had thousands of fans doing the sort of mental isometrics that take place only with unforeseen sporting success or a pop quiz in algebra.

If the M's play .500 ball the rest of the way, how many victories will they have at the end of the season?

On May 1, the answer was 88, and since 90 to 95 wins are usually sufficient for securing a playoff berth – the Atlanta Braves won the National League East this year with exactly 88 victories – the early implications to any longtime Mariners fan were thrilling. And a little disorienting.

If the M's can win 15 games a month from here on out, they'll have 95 victories. Whoa!

True, the springtime musings of a desperate baseball fan are as rational as those of a guest on "Jerry Springer." The M's had never won more than 91 games in a season, and they had managed to never do that with teams that scored a lot of runs.

Sure enough, the computation festival seemed premature as the Mariners began May by winning three games and losing four. Perhaps hoping for .500 ball the rest of the season was a little too greedy.

And perhaps not. A month passed before the Mariners lost four more games. By mid-June they were 49-13, having reeled off winning streaks of eight, nine and 15 games. With a hundred games left in the season, the calculations of even the most arithmetically challenged started to make perfectly good sense.

If the M's go 50 and 50 from now on, they'll have 99 victories. Yikes!

Clearly, this team was not normal.

AS THEY LEFT spring training at the end of March, the Mariners looked breathtakingly normal. Having made it to the American League Championship Series the year before, they easily engendered hope in the heart of the average fan, regardless of super shortstop Alex Rodriguez's departure for greener pastures. But they were a team of mostly seasoned veterans who had won 13 and lost 19 in a not-so-splendid spring campaign. A good team? Maybe. But a great team? A team that would end up sharing the major league record for victories in a season? Anyone who harbored such thoughts needed some serious remedial reading of the tea leaves.

Even general manager Pat Gillick thought the Mariners could use another brawny bat in the line-up and a take-charge starter on the mound. Most of the experts who spend six weeks in Arizona or Florida working on their oracular skills predicted the Mariners for second or third place in the American League West. The Oakland A's were the class of the division, they said. The Texas Rangers, after giving A-Rod enough cash to tide him over for a millennium of weekends, looked like a contender too, even if their pitching was spottier than a detergent commercial.

The Mariners did have this new import named Ichiro Suzuki, a wisp of a leadoff hitter who had won seven batting titles in Japan. In a row. But even if he was the most gifted table-setter since Martha Stewart, did the Mariners have enough oomph in the lineup behind him? Edgar Martinez and John Olerud were bona fide run producers, sure. But Mike Cameron? Bret Boone? David Bell?

Without A-Rod and the dourly departed Ken Griffey Jr. knocking balls over the fence, could a decent pitching staff expect any offensive support at all?

The answer was soon apparent. In their first 15 games, the Mariners' opponents averaged a respectable four runs per game. But the Mariners averaged five and a half.

Over the next 15, the Mariners displayed the remarkable consistency that would become their hallmark in a historic season, continuing to average 5.5 runs a game while their opponents' average dropped to three. The Mariners' hitting was not only good, it was astonishingly productive; the pitching was not only good, it was downright dominant. In mid-June, M's broadcaster Dave Niehaus, who has been with the team since it set sail in 1977, was prompted to say: "Enjoy the ride. You may never see anything like it again."

AT THE ALL-STAR break in July, Niehaus was looking like a prophet and the Mariners were looking for a challenge. They were so far ahead of the second-place A's — 19 games — that the division title was deemed a lock by all but the faint-hearted. They were on a pace to win 117 games. The irrepressible Ichiro, who could hit a baseball with aplomb or a plumb bob, was the talk of baseball. Boone, in his second tour as a Mariner, was having a season that made it easy to forget Alex Whatsisname. Pitchers Freddy Garcia and Aaron Sele already had 10 victories. Jamie Moyer had

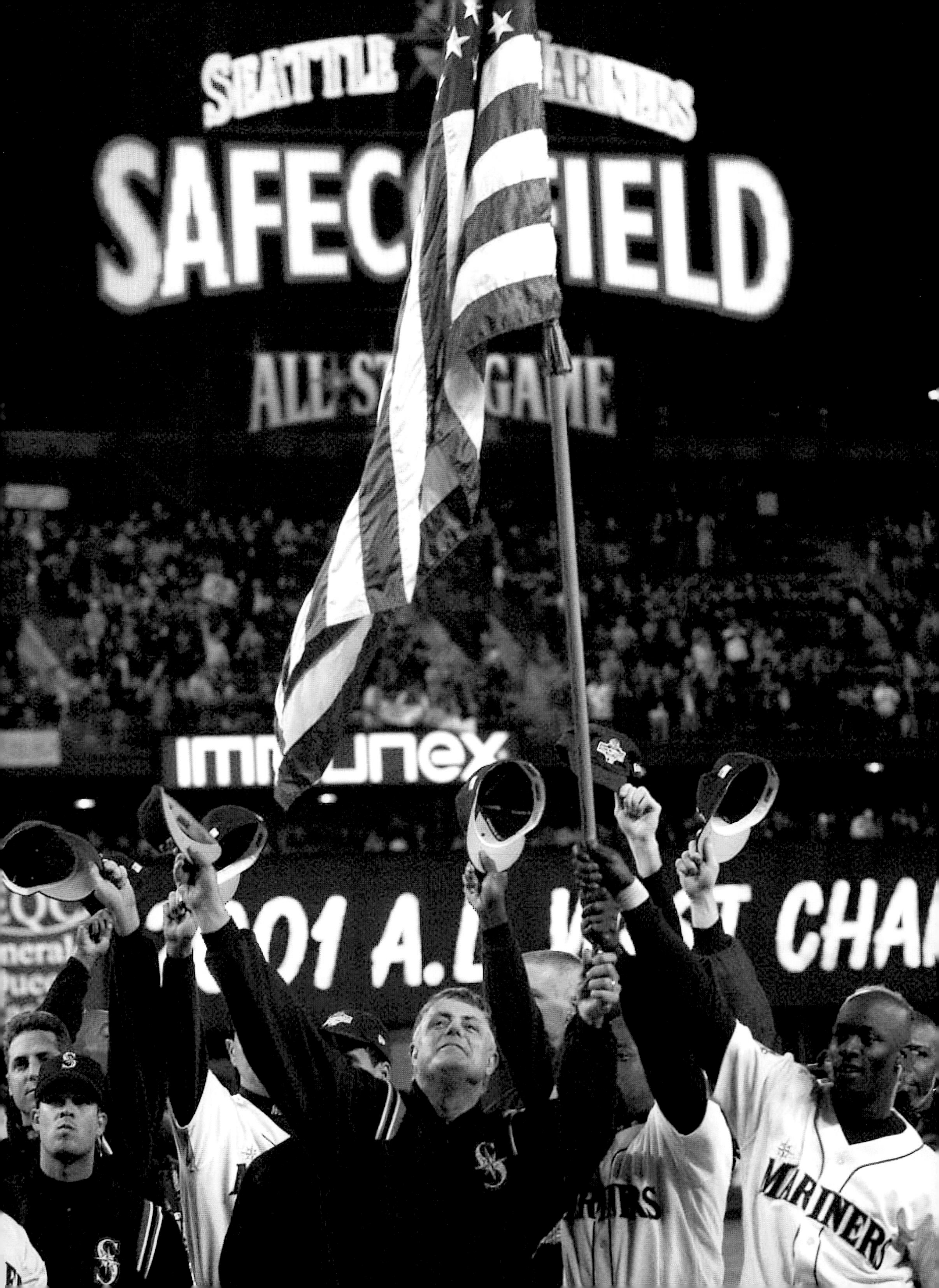
SEATTLE MARINERS
ALL-STAR GAME
IMMUNEX
MARINERS
MARINERS

nine. Paul Abbott, who missed most of April with a sore shoulder, had seven.

And what about that bullpen? Teams quickly learned that if they didn't score early, they would face a corps of relievers that gave up runs the way a post office gives up parking spaces. Ryan Franklin, Jeff Nelson and Arthur Lee Rhodes routinely shut down the opposition, giving way to Kazuhiro Sasaki for the finishing touché in the ninth inning.

In accordance with the improbable script that was unfolding, Team Terrific placed eight players on the American League All-Star team: Martinez, Olerud, Boone, Ichiro, Garcia, Sasaki, Nelson and Cameron, the Mariners' unofficial ambassador of smiles. Sele and Rhodes also had All-Star credentials, and Bell was second in the voting for All-Star third basemen, but the rules state that all teams must have representation, so some Mariners had to stay home.

Actually, all the Mariners got to stay home. The sporting deities had already ordained that Seattle's Safeco Field was to be the site of baseball's summer showcase. Why not? In this most unlikely of seasons, it was fitting that the Mariners and their city share the world stage. Just as fittingly, since this was a team of players reluctant to have attention directed at any one individual, they graciously let the All-Star spotlight shine on Baltimore's Cal Ripken, who hit a home run in his final appearance as an All-Star and was named the game's most valuable player. (For the record, the Mariners made some contribu-

tions. Garcia got the victory and Sasaki got the save, the first time teammates have done that in an All-Star game. Nelson pitched a scoreless seventh inning and Ichiro and Cameron had base hits.)

THE MARINERS' TANGO with the implausible continued through August and into September. On Labor Day, they recorded their 99th victory, prompting a new round of cerebral ciphering among fans who never dreamed these guys could hit triple figures. At that point, no other team in either league had reached 85 wins. Seattle's lead over Oakland, the hottest team in the majors after the All-Star break, had dwindled only a game, from 19 to 18.

A week later, the Mariners were poised to clinch the American League West championship. If they could beat the Angels on Sept. 11 and the Rangers could beat the A's, the division crown was Seattle's. But the game – that particular game *and* the general abstraction of baseball as America's pastime – was rendered meaningless by the terrorist attacks on the World Trade Center and the Pentagon. Playing baseball was not only irrelevant, it was almost irreverent.

When Major League Baseball resumed play after a seven-day hiatus, Safeco Field seemed like a different place. Security was tightened. Emotions were subdued. The most popular banner was now the American flag. For the seventh-inning stretch, "Take Me Out to the Ballgame" and "Louie,

Lou Piniella and his players stand united under the flag after clinching the American League West championship. The celebration was tempered by memories of September 11. PHOTOGRAPH BY PAUL KITAGAKI JR.

"It's only baseball," Jennifer Wallner
seems to be saying as she tries to
cheer up her date, Adam Karl.
The Mariners had just lost Game 2
of the American League
Championship Series to the Yankees.
PHOTOGRAPH BY MIKE URBAN

Louie" had taken a back seat to "America the Beautiful."

The Mariners clinched the AL West on Sept. 19 with a 5-0 shutout of the Angels. What happened next left tear ducts empty throughout the Northwest and the M's bandwagon crammed with late arrivals who might have been waiting for a genuine reason to believe. Rather than swarm the field and thump on each other like overdeveloped schoolchildren, the Mariners made a quiet procession around the infield. Led by Mark McLemore, who held aloft the Stars and Stripes, the players knelt at the pitcher's mound, said a prayer and then acknowledged the fans, who cheered and wept at the same time.

In a world desperate for something to hold dear, the Mariners' touching display of class and dignity reminded everyone that this was a special team.

"It goes to show you," manager Lou Piniella would say later, "that when a group of men are committed to getting something done and play together as a team and stay together and root for each other and play hard every day, good things happen."

SO MANY GOOD things happened to the Mariners in 2001 that the record book has more new entries than Ichiro's long list of interview requests. From individual achievements to team milestones to fan turnout to TV ratings that went through the Safeco Field roof, it was something to appreciate.

"This just doesn't happen," Niehaus said as the regular season came to an end in early October. "It's been a fantasy."

Though hardly essential in the preservation of municipal underpinnings, it was most welcome as a vitamin supplement for the civic psyche. Aside from restaurateurs who suffered empty establishments whenever the Mariners played, the Northwest embraced the team simply because it succeeded. It's hard not to love a team that wins 70 percent of the time.

But when we've moved on down the road and are looking back on the 116 victories and the innumerable records matched or broken, we'll remember a team that also inspired us with hard work, dedication, professionalism, consistency, nobility.

"It hasn't been as easy as it looks," Piniella said on the night the Mariners clinched the AL West.

Failing to reach the World Series made the validity of that statement painfully obvious. But even in the disappointment of dropping the American League Championship Series to the New York Yankees in five games, the Mariners could take satisfaction in knowing they brought immeasurable joy to Seattle for six months, spreading it beyond the usual confines to people who knew little about baseball but a lot about how much fun it is to live in a community bursting with pride.

THE FORMULA

LEADERSHIP
Under Lincoln, all M's are equal

NOW THAT THE Mariners have two premier Japanese players, in addition to the Japanese-led franchise ownership, it might not be too long before manager Lou Piniella is outfitted for his sumo belt.

Imagine Piniella in the ring against Don Zimmer. It would be on a par with Godzilla vs. Rodan – a pop-culture event of worldwide irresistibility.

But let's pull back from the ridiculous to a more sublime Japanese influence on the Mariners.

"I learned something from Mr. (Minoru) Arakawa," club CEO Howard Lincoln said in March about his former boss at Nintendo, the video game maker and largest Mariners owner. "It's important to treat all employees equally, and that applies to sports as well as business."

The subject came up because the Mariners, for the first time since Ken Griffey Jr. came to the majors in 1989, are without a dominant clubhouse figure. They also are without a big bopper – an obvious No. 3 hitter after having been blessed for more than a decade with Griffey and Alex Rodriguez.

When Lincoln said that the Mariners don't need superstars to succeed, the thought occurred that they might be putting a premium on wonderfulness instead of winning. But Lincoln believes there is a compromise position and that self-absorbed jerkism becomes a problem only when allowed to fester.

In his years with law firms as well as at Nintendo, Lincoln said he had to make the call on numerous employees who didn't get it. Nor will he hesitate with the Mariners.

So far he hasn't been tested, he said. Randy Johnson was gone and Griffey was on his way out when Lincoln was taking over. Rodriguez, despite the unpleasant outcome of his Seattle career, was not a problem.

Griffey, it should be pointed out, was never a bad guy, just moody and cantankerous. And because he was in Seattle longer than everyone in ownership and all but a handful of front office staffers and players, he believed himself entitled to do some franchise steering.

There is none of that now in the clubhouse. Nor is there likely to be in the foreseeable future. Lincoln is seeing to it that no one is bigger than the franchise.

–Art Thiel

HOWARD LINCOLN SET THE TONE FOR A TEAM WITH NO SUPERSTARS – AND NO SUPERSTAR ATTITUDE.

Lou Piniella made the most of abundant speed, pitching, defense and surprising hitting to steer the M's to a record unsurpassed in 130 years of professional baseball.

PHOTOGRAPH BY
DAN DeLONG

AS PINIELLA GROWS, SO DO HIS MARINERS

THE GLIB REACTION when Lou Piniella signed a three-year deal with the Mariners last November was one of relief:

Finally, someone wants to stay!

After Randy Johnson, after Ken Griffey Jr., after Alex Rodriguez, the Mariners organization had maintained important continuity. It had retained a familiar face and a dominant personality from an era in which the Mariners emerged from 18 seasons of futility and were reborn winners.

But that only scratches the surface. Piniella deserves credit for more than merely being the one who decided to stay.

In fact, through the turmoil that followed the stunning 1995 season – when Johnson was traded, when a new stadium's construction strained community goodwill, when Griffey, the former face of the Mariners, asked to be traded – it was Piniella who ingrained himself in the organization and in Seattle.

Piniella endured the transition from the Kingdome to Safeco Field.

Piniella survived a major transition in ownership.

Piniella oversaw the transition from long ball to "situational baseball."

Piniella helped navigate a so-called small-market franchise to the Mariners' current status as one of baseball's top eight franchises.

Piniella, after winning AL West titles in 1995 and '97, rose again with teams of an entirely different sort, first competing with the Yankees through six games of the American League Championship Series in 2000 and then tying the major league record for victories in 2001.

After the 1999 season, when general manager Pat Gillick was signed, owner Howard Lincoln assumed new duties as chief executive and Piniella's old friend Woody Woodward went into early retirement, Piniella chose not to sign a long-term deal. Instead, he took stock of what was happening in the organization.

The results startled everyone, Piniella included. The team was better, more aggressive, more professional, more hungry than anyone would have guessed. It took on the personality of its manager.

– Laura Vecsey

Paul Abbott (above) started the season on the disabled list with a stiff shoulder but limbered up enough to get a career-high 17 victories and the league's second-best win percentage.

PHOTOGRAPH BY MIKE URBAN

PITCHING
Starters and relievers put it all together

JULY COMES TO an end today. Coming with it is the trading deadline. Coming with it, too, is the end of one of the most remarkable runs of pitching in Seattle history.

The Mariners have played 26 games in July. Six times the pitching staff has thrown shutouts. Twice more the pitchers have allowed one run. Five times the Mariners have allowed just two runs.

That's 13 games in which the Mariners have surrendered two or fewer runs.

Small wonder the Mariners have maintained their blistering pace in the American League West. Oakland has gone 18-8 in July but hasn't been able to pick up a single game in the standings.

"We know the pitching staff is going to keep us in every game," second baseman Bret Boone said. "The great thing about that is that we know we don't have the pressure to score a lot of runs every night."

Not that the Mariners can't score. Seattle's offensive output is down a little since the All-Star break, but the Mariners still lead the major leagues in scoring. They lead the majors in defense, too. Somehow, however, it always seems to come back to the pitching.

"Everybody's in a good rhythm right now," pitching coach Bryan Price said. "It's become a matter of guys avoiding the things that make them

Homegrown starter Aaron Sele from Poulsbo went 8-0 for the best season start in Mariners history.

PHOTOGRAPH BY DAN DeLONG

susceptible to giving up big innings."

For a power pitcher like Freddy Garcia, it's a matter of keeping the ball in the park. He's allowed one homer in his past seven starts.

For a breaking ball pitcher like Aaron Sele, it's a matter of having command of his curve and the ability to keep it down at the knees.

For a finesse pitcher like Jamie Moyer, it's a matter of releasing the changeup so that it looks like a fastball. Until the batter screws himself into the ground trying to swing at it.

For a closer like Kazuhiro Sasaki, it's a matter of having his forkball drop off the table just as the batter gets on it.

For a closer-in-training like Jose Paniagua, it's a matter of keeping the walk totals down and the strikeout totals up.

In short, each Mariners pitcher has a different key. But in one regard, they are all alike.

"It's a matter of each guy throwing smart pitches," Price said. "You know a guy has matured into the role when he can throw with his head and not just with his heart."

Last August, the Mariners' pitching failed. Manager Lou Piniella seems confident that no repeat is in the offing.

"Part of that was guys were worn out a little in the heat of the summer," Piniella said. "That's not the case now. We've been able to rest everybody a lot. We had relievers early in the year on the way to 90-game seasons. We've cut that back. Everybody is rested, everybody is confident, and people all know their roles. It makes for a good situation."

One that is the envy of baseball.

"When you get behind against this team," Twins pitcher Eric Milton said, "it's pretty much impossible to come back."

– John Hickey

Set-up men Arthur Rhodes
(above) and Jeff Nelson were
big reasons why Seattle's
bullpen was second to none.
PHOTOGRAPHS BY
PAUL KITAGAKI JR.

Kazuhiro Sasaki
followed his Rookie
of the Year season
with an All-Star
appearance and 45
saves, eight more
than his own
team record.
PHOTOGRAPH BY
PAUL KITAGAKI JR.

GREAT ROTATIONS

1920 WHITE SOX

Red Faber	23-13
Lefty Williams	22-14
Dickie Kerr	21-9
Ed Cicotte	21-10

1931 ATHLETICS

Lefty Grove	31-4
George Earnshaw	21-7
Rube Walberg	20-12
Roy Mahaffey	15-4

1954 INDIANS

Bob Lemon	23-7
Early Wynn	23-11
Mike Garcia	19-8
Art Houtteman	15-7
Bob Feller	12-3

1968 CARDINALS

Bob Gibson	22-9
Nelson Briles	19-11
Ray Washburn	14-8
Steve Carlton	13-11

1971 ORIOLES

Dave McNally	21-5
Pat Dobson	20-8
Jim Palmer	20-9
Mike Cuellar	20-9

1986 METS

Bob Ojeda	18-5
Dwight Gooden	17-6
Sid Fernandez	16-6
Ron Darling	15-6

2001 MARINERS

Jamie Moyer	20-6
Freddy Garcia	18-6
Paul Abbott	17-4
Aaron Sele	15-5

Two mainstays in the middle of the league's best defense were Carlos Guillen (left), who played his first season as Seattle's shortstop, and catcher Dan Wilson, a steadying influence behind the plate.

PHOTOGRAPHS BY DAN DeLONG
AND PAUL KITAGAKI JR.

DEFENSE
With speed and steadiness comes greatness in the field

ICHIRO SUZUKI STOOD in right field during batting practice on a June day at Safeco Field, stretching and shagging fly balls.

As once such ball approached, Ichiro casually bent forward at the waist, as if to bow. With his hands at his sides, he cocked his left wrist and caught the ball at the small of his back. It earned one of the few standing ovations for fielding in batting practice history.

They have done it with the flash of Ichiro's outfield wizardry, and they have done it with the quiet steadiness of shortstop Carlos Guillen. Although it sometimes gets lost among offensive fireworks and gaudy pitching records, the Mariners have played the best defense in the American League.

"We've got a great defensive team – not just good, great," second baseman Bret Boone said. "It's as good as I've seen anywhere, for anybody, and certainly the best I've ever played on."

As with many areas of their game this season, the Mariners are succeeding on defense not with star power, but with consistently solid play around the field.

The Mariners have three Gold Glove winners:

First baseman John Olerud in 2000, outfielder Jay Buhner in 1996 and Boone in 1998. Boone fans will tell you he was robbed of the award in 1995 and '96, when he led the National League in fielding percentage.

Perhaps the key to the 2001 success was, ironically, the departure of All-Star and standout defensive shortstop Alex Rodriguez. It allowed Guillen, who committed 21 errors last season playing mostly third base, to take over at shortstop, his natural position. That gave David Bell the full-time third base job, putting him at his natural position. That sent the Mariners after a second baseman, returning Boone to Seattle. That pried Mark McLemore free from second base and into a roving backup role that has been extremely successful.

"Mac is a guy that does it with his athletic ability," Bell said. "That amazes me. There's no way many players could go from left field to third base to second base, and make it look easy. That's the thing about good defensive players. They make plays look routine that really are difficult."

– David Andriesen

THE FORMULA

"FROM DAVID BELL TO JOHN OLERUD, THOSE GUYS ARE PLAYING LIKE THE GREAT WALL OF CHINA.
YOU CAN'T GET ANYTHING THROUGH THERE." – Mike Cameron

Shortstop Mark McLemore (above) makes a diving catch in front of center fielder Mike Cameron. McLemore played shortstop after Carlos Guillen was diagnosed with tuberculosis in September.

A third generation big-leaguer, David Bell (left) played Gold Glove-caliber defense at third base.

PHOTOGRAPHS BY PAUL KITAGAKI JR.

Center fielder Mike Cameron leaps high to take a home run away from Detroit's Tony Clark, giving fans in the bleachers reason to marvel.

PHOTOGRAPH BY

"WE DON'T HAVE ANY BIG EGOS IN THIS OFFENSE. WE JUST GO OUT AND HIT." – Bret Boone

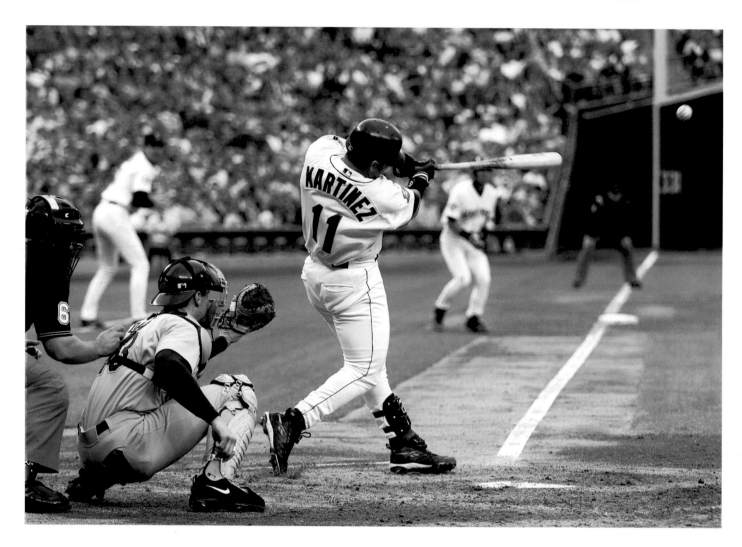

HITTING
Perry helps turn perceived weakness into a strength

Designated hitter Edgar Martinez connects for a two-run double, epitomizing the Mariners' relentlessly efficient offense. They led the American League in batting average and the majors in runs.

PHOTOGRAPH BY
PAUL KITAGAKI JR.

THE OLDER WE get, the saying goes, the better we were. That goes for former major leaguers as well.

"He's a way better hitter now than he was when he played," Mariners outfielder Al Martin cracks about hitting coach Gerald Perry. "I can't wait to see how good I'm going to be when I retire."

Perry has little need to embellish his playing career. He was on the field for 13 years with Atlanta, Kansas City and St. Louis. He stole 42 bases for the 1987 Braves and was an All-Star in 1988, when he led major league first basemen with a .300 average. He hit a grand slam off Nolan Ryan.

But the legend of the 40-year-old Georgia native, who retired as a player after the 1995 season, is growing in his second season as instructor, mentor and psychologist for Mariners hitters.

Seattle is running away with the American League West, and the team that was supposed to have so many holes on offense leads the major leagues in runs scored. The Mariners are in the top three in batting average and on-base percentage. No American League team draws more walks or hits more sacrifice flies, and no team in the majors grounds into fewer double plays.

"I think when you look at the success of our club offensively, a good portion of the credit should

Ichiro Suzuki kept getting hits and Bret Boone kept driving in runs. Both newcomers had historic roles in Seattle's record-breaking year.

PHOTOGRAPHS BY PAUL KITAGAKI JR.

go to Gerald," manager Lou Piniella said. "He's mainly responsible for it."

Players praise Perry for his work ethic and approachability, his equal treatment of everyone on the roster and for being able to sense when a hitter needs help, or just needs to be left alone to work through a problem.

"He's got a watchful eye on guys," said catcher Dan Wilson, one of several hitters who has shown marked improvement. "If you do come to him, he's more than willing to help, but he's always giving you little things. If he's got a hot spot with you, something you need to pay attention to, he's going to keep reminding you of it, but not in a negative way."

"The first thing you've got to do to be successful is be able to communicate with the players," Piniella said. "That's essential for any coach. And you have to earn their confidence and their respect. Gerald's done that."

Every player is scrutinized in game situations, batting practice and on videotape. Perry reviews tapes extensively with video coordinator Carl Hamilton to pick up tendencies among his hitters, and no player escapes his attention.

Perry deflects much of the credit to other coaches and a hard-working group of players, but admits he's enjoying the team's success.

"It's a rewarding job," he said. "I'm very satisfied when the guys are having success, and probably more upset than they are when they're not.

"This team works their tails off, day in and day out. We don't have any jerks on the team. They're all good guys, and they go at it every day with everything they have to offer."

The same can be said of their hitting coach.

– David Andriesen

VERSATILITY
Nobody does more than six-position McLemore

THE NEXT PERSON to say "doing the little things" in reference to the Mariners deserves to be drawn, quartered, chilled and served with a slice of lemon.

It's not a matter of accuracy. It's just that in this extraordinary season, such an insight has the observational punch of noting that a poke in the eye hurts.

Most of all, don't say it about Mark McLemore. He might get irritated – and perhaps justifiably so. He does so many little things that's it's actually a big thing, because he does everything.

Hyperbole is overstatement to make a point. That's not happening here. It's fair to assert that McLemore plays more positions well – six this season – than any other player in the American League.

Need an outfielder? Gotcha covered, in every direction. Infield? He's played them all except first base and behind the dish. Designated hitter? He's done that too. Bat him first, second, ninth – whatever – it doesn't matter.

How about some speed-created havoc on the basepaths?

Against the Baltimore Orioles in May,

McLemore tied a team record with four stolen bases in one game. He swiped 39 this year, eclipsing his career high of 30 set just last season. He had 59 RBIs for the season, making it the second most productive of his 13-year career.

McLemore went into the postseason as the Mariners' starting shortstop, which doesn't sound that special, unless you remember the veteran hadn't lined up there in more than a decade before this season.

"He's done a heck of a job playing all over the field," manager Lou Piniella said. "For him to have played shortstop as well as he has is something special."

When he played with the Texas Rangers in 1995, McLemore was the only American League player to start 50 or more games in both the infield and outfield. But he hasn't received that much attention during his career, in large part because of seven stints on the disabled list previous to last year.

"It's not a high-profile thing he does," second baseman Bret Boone said. "But he's been a very unsung hero."

– Ted Miller

While playing wherever he was needed in the field, Mark McLemore also was valuable as a No. 2 hitter, capable of advancing the runner or delivering a clutch hit.

PHOTOGRAPH BY GILBER W. ARIAS

Showing one reason why he's a fan favorite, Mike Cameron signs autographs during All-Star Game workouts at Safeco Field.

PHOTOGRAPH BY PAUL KITAGAKI JR.

PERSONALITY

Joyous Cameron connects with an adoring public

MIKE CAMERON HAS a fantastic signature, a big, looping script that he crafts carefully each time, finishing with a neat "44" underneath.

In terms of value, however, Cameron's autograph is lousy. The darn thing is everywhere.

"I just try to schedule in time for it every day," he says of his pregame autograph sessions. "The fans inspire me. They're a huge reason for my success. I enjoy doing it, really."

Is this guy for real? Is Mike Cameron not only a wall-climbing, hard-hitting, basepath-blazing center fielder, but also the front-runner for Nicest Guy in Baseball? The answer, apparently, is yes.

"That's not for show. That's reality. He's a nice guy, period," Mariners teammate Mark McLemore said. "He has fun, he enjoys life and he enjoys the game. He's one of the best-liked players throughout the league."

Before a recent game, the 28-year-old from LaGrange, Ga., sat on a concrete dugout step at Safeco Field, putting a black Sharpie through its paces. Each time Cameron looked up to the crowd of mostly children behind the dugout, it would rain caps, baseballs, shirts, gloves and programs. And each time, he gathered up the items, signed them meticulously – with his left hand, notable because he bats and throws right-handed – and threw them on top of the dugout to be retrieved.

Among the projectiles were Cameron T-shirts given away at an earlier game. It might not have been a red-letter day on your calendar, but certainly was on his.

"Mike Cameron T-shirt Day. Unbelievable."

"That's something to be proud of, it really is," manager Lou Piniella said. "It goes to show you what the organization thinks of him."

When Cameron first saw one of the giveaway shirts during batting practice, he promptly put the youth-size shirt on – over both his uniform and a sweatshirt. Looking like a deformed sausage in its casing, he puffed up his chest and walked over to a group behind the batting cage, causing Ichiro Suzuki to double over with laughter.

Although you won't find it in his contract, making Ichiro laugh is one of Cameron's jobs.

"They're good friends," Piniella said. "They locker next to each other, and with all the media attention that Ichiro gets, Cameron's a good diversion for him."

"I just try to keep him loose and make him feel comfortable," Cameron said. "He's the engine of our train, and as long as the engine of our train is feeling comfortable, we're going to be pretty successful."

Besides, entertaining Ichiro is hardly a burdensome assignment. Cameron rarely misses an opportunity to goof, strut, needle and flash his megawatt smile.

"He's got a great attitude and it helps us, it really does," Piniella said. "He's very positive and he goes out and plays hard every day. It's infectious.

"He's won the fans over because of the way he's conducted himself both on and off the field. He's a good young man and he's a good player."

– David Andriesen

IS THIS GUY FOR REAL? IS MIKE CAMERON NOT ONLY A WALL-CLIMBING, HARD-HITTING, BASEPATH-BLAZING CENTER FIELDER, BUT ALSO THE FRONT-RUNNER FOR NICEST GUY IN BASEBALL? THE ANSWER, APPARENTLY, IS YES.

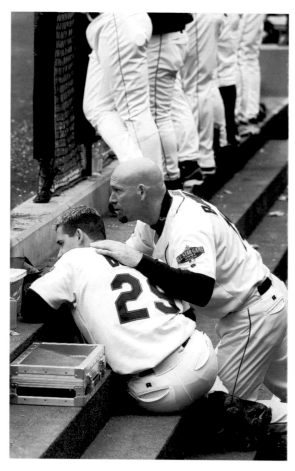

Clubhouse leader Jay Buhner consoles slumping
teammate Bret Boone during the division playoffs
and keeps things loose during the regular season,
looking for suspects for his kangaroo court.

PHOTOGRAPHS BY MIKE URBAN AND GILBERT W. ARIAS

INSPIRATION
Even while injured, Buhner finds ways to contribute

**"HE'S A
GREAT
EXAMPLE
FOR ALL OF
US."**
– Paul Abbott

RIGHT FIELD HAS become known as Area 51
this season after the uniform number of Ichiro
Suzuki, but yesterday, during Buhner Buzz Night, it
was once again the Bone Yard, home of bald guys
and inflatable bones paying tribute to injured outfielder Jay Buhner.

"He's still here," pitcher Paul Abbott said. "If his
name wasn't over his locker over there, there
would be a big void in this clubhouse. He's like a
security blanket."

"He's such an important presence and a great
teammate," first baseman John Olerud said. "He's
there when someone is down or not playing well or
made a mistake. He's always encouraging, and
that's not the easiest thing to do sometimes."

His 305 career home runs are second in franchise history, but Buhner's most valuable contribution might be his leadership in the clubhouse. He is
relentlessly positive, eager to address issues and
respected by all. He is the presiding officer of the
team's kangaroo court and the chief assignor of
nicknames.

A bum foot has not affected his ability to help
the team off the field. He rejoined the team on a
day-to-day basis in May and resumed traveling on
road trips. He's studying pitchers, taking a lot of
medical treatment and trying not to lose patience.
In the meantime, he continues to be a positive force
in a very positive clubhouse.

– David Andriesen

THE STANDOUTS

ICHIRO
Sensation from Japan captures the imagination of a city

THIS STORY DOES not reveal the key to Ichiro's soul, or even his game.

You will not read about how Ichiro carries a lock of Ted Williams' hair in a locket around his neck, or that the reason he momentarily holds his bat straight up and down in front of him before setting his stance is that it's an inspirational gesture to honor his father.

If those things were true, if there were a story of such poignancy and revelation, you would know it by now. It would have been told, retold, embellished and made into a Japanese animated TV special.

Dozens of people have spent the better part of a decade chronicling Ichiro and trying to probe his psyche. Given the general failure of those efforts at insight, it might be time to consider the possibility that the Mariners right fielder, who caused a superlative shortage on two continents by electrifying the U.S. major leagues this season, is a regular guy from Kasugai who just happens to be one of the best baseball players on the planet.

"I only want to play baseball," said the one-name wonder, and you get the feeling that for Ichiro it is not a throwaway response but a mantra.

It is through playing baseball – and only through playing baseball – that the 27-year-old became the biggest story in baseball after making the jump from Japan's Pacific League, where he won seven consecutive batting titles.

Unlike Michael Jordan or Tiger Woods, Ichiro is without an off-field persona to fuel his image. America doesn't yet have a sense of what kind of guy Ichiro is. There have been no heartfelt ESPN interviews, no late nights on the town, no dating of Anna Kournikova.

But his game? Now *that* has personality. It's downright charismatic.

He doesn't walk. He doesn't strike out. He's halfway to first base before fans in the outfield hear the crack of the bat. He seems to have the same approach as the guys in your rec softball league: Put the ball in play and run like mad.

But however unconventional and even haphazard he might look to the untrained eye, he can hit a baseball with a precision rarely seen in the game's history. He punches the ball to all fields, seemingly wherever he wants it, pushing countless singles just past outstretched gloves of fielders.

The next time Ichiro hits a triple, watch him run. He has not so much a gait as a glide, his torso not bobbing up and down with his steps but seemingly floating around the bases. It is a telltale sign of a natural athlete.

If his bat were his only tool, Ichiro would be amazing enough. But his arm, glove, speed and all-around smart play are equally impressive.

What might be most intriguing is his ability to seemingly turn it on when it matters most. With the bases empty this season, Ichiro hit .313. Put a runner in scoring position and his average jumped to .449 – nearly 30 points higher than any other American League player. Up the ante, making it two out with runners in scoring position, and he hit .468.

"He's fun to watch," second baseman Bret Boone said. "The sucker can hit."

— David Andriesen

Ichiro at the plate is a picture of precision, each time starting with the bat held straight up in front of him and sighting through it, as if taking aim at the pitcher. PHOTOGRAPH BY PAUL KITAGAKI JR.

Bolting from the batter's box, Ichiro uses his quickness to turn routine grounders into infield hits. His speed helped him get 242 hits, the most by any player since 1930.

PHOTOGRAPH BY
PAUL KITAGAKI JR.

RACING FOR RECORDS

NOT IN SEATTLE'S 25 years in the major leagues has there been a hitter who can get mothers to pause while fixing dinner, fathers to halt channel surfing and ballpark patrons to scurry back from beer lines, just to witness an infield grounder.

Even teammates climb to the top steps of the dugout to watch Ichiro Suzuki burn worms.

Ichiro did not invent stick-handling, nor did he invent small ball. But the suspicion grows that the game has seen few more adroit practitioners of the electric grounder. For a baseball citizenry drunk for a decade on home runs, the development has been a revelation.

– Art Thiel

From the first day of spring training, the Japanese media had Ichiro covered.

PHOTOGRAPH BY PAUL KITAGAKI JR.

HITTING NEW HEIGHTS

ICHIRO'S PRESENCE AT or near the top of so many American League offensive categories in his rookie major league season was incredible.

Everyone understood the seven-time batting champion from Japan could make an impact in America. Mets manager Bobby Valentine pushed his general manager to outbid the Mariners for the rights to negotiate with the Orix Blue Wave for Ichiro.

But that Ichiro took his hitting to these heights, at this stage, against a slew of pitchers he had never seen, in ballparks he had never played in and under travel conditions he had never experienced – well, that is surreal.

– Laura Vecsey

Ichiro didn't walk or strike out often. What he did was make contact. The result was an American League batting championship and records galore.

PHOTOGRAPH BY MIKE URBAN

The Ichiro bobblehead doll became an instant collector's item.

Ichiro rolls after diving to make a spectacular catch of a line drive by Arizona's Luis Gonzalez. The Mariners right fielder won respect for his defense as much as his hitting.

PHOTOGRAPH BY
MIKE URBAN

SOMETHING SPECIAL

HERE IS THE one thing about Ichiro, besides – but not apart from – his arm, speed, batting average, All-Star votes, faint sideburns and right-sleeve tug:

Fearlessness.

As a rookie from a baseball nation that had never exported a position player, Ichiro walked over to major league baseball and put his foot on its throat.

Pedro Martinez, Yankee Stadium, cross-county travel, gut-bomb fast food, teammates with two new languages … none of it mattered.

From the first game, Ichiro became the best player on the best team, a team chasing history as well as a championship. For an almost jockey-sized player who employs the 100-foot single as his primary weapon, Ichiro's absence of apprehension was a wonder but not much of a mystery – he was the first rookie in All-Star Game history to lead fan balloting.

Talent wasn't as much a question as was Ichiro's approach to the big, bad world of American ball. The conventional assumption was of a learning curve, an adjustment time, a graduation of expectations.

Wrong.

Right away, he was his own man, unflinchingly putting himself on his own spot.

He told Lou Piniella he wasn't hitting third in the lineup, as the manager was considering. Nor would his unorthodox swing be altered for the allegedly more powerful major league pitchers. Nor would he demonstrate in spring training his ability to pull the ball to right field, despite Piniella's insistence, which led to this surprising retort on the field.

"I'm just setting 'em up," Ichiro said, referring to opposing pitchers. "No problem."

Ichiro hit .336 in April, .379 in May and .339 in June. For most of the season, he was at or near the top of the American League leaders in hits, runs, average, at-bats, stolen bases and singles that miss fielding leather by an inch.

All of the forecasted obstacles – culture, food, travel, pitching – proved manageable, in part because Ichiro had no fear of any of them.

– Art Thiel

KEEPING IT SIMPLE

AFTER BANGING OUT six hits in nine at-bats in a two-game stretch against the Red Sox, Ichiro dismissed any notion of mastery over Boston, or of hitting.

"I just have," he said, "a wider strike zone."

The secret was thus revealed – Ichiro accepts without complaint the notion that any pitch within the lash of his bat is a strike, and therefore must be put in play.

It's a simple concept. But few American batters have displayed either the courage or the skill to implement it.

Ichiro's midseason falloff from a pace that reached .371 was attributed by some to opponents finally getting a notion of how to pitch to him. Breaking stuff away, fastballs in.

For a time, the strategy was working. Whether it was because he succumbed to many American hitters' habit of pulling every pitch, or whether he was seduced by manager Lou Piniella's joke about inserting him in the Home Run Derby before the All-Star Game, Ichiro wasn't making contact the same way he showed in April and May.

But by August he once again was punching outside breaking balls to left and showing bunts more

Ichiro throws from right field over Mike Cameron. Runners rarely challenged his arm.

PHOTOGRAPH BY DAN DeLONG

frequently, forcing the third baseman to play closer to the plate, opening the shortstop hole wider.

The increasing frequency of his presence on base renewed the distractions for the defense, which only was a help to the No. 2 hitter.

"I can't really tell you what he's doing differently," Mark McLemore said. "All I know is, I'm having a lot of fun hitting in the two hole."

– Art Thiel

A blur on the base paths, Ichiro gave defenses one more thing to worry about. He led the major leagues with 56 stolen bases.

PHOTOGRAPH BY GRANT M. HALLER

Ichiro acknowledges a standing ovation at Safeco Field after breaking the 90-year-old major league rookie record for hits in a season.

PHOTOGRAPH BY RENEE C. BYER

Two Seattle second graders hug their hero on Mariners Education Day at John Stanford International School.

PHOTOGRAPH BY DAN DeLONG

WIZARD OF AHS

THE MORE ICHIRO was asked about the feat – 200 hits with 30 games left in the season – the more he warmed up to his accomplishment.

"Of course, I am amazed myself," he said. "When I look back from where I started, I didn't think of any numbers to achieve."

That's where hitting coach Gerald Perry ratted Ichiro out.

"Back in spring training, he had this as a goal," Perry said.

Caught in the apparent contradiction, Ichiro just smiled slyly. Meanwhile, his teammates were falling over themselves talking about the achievement.

"It's tremendous to get 200 hits, especially with a month to go in the season," Mike Cameron said. "But it's not surprising. We know what a great approach he has at the plate, what a great swing. Ichiro gets hits when nobody else would even think about getting hits."

Cameron doesn't see things getting better for pitchers in the American League.

"The crazy thing is that they can't pitch him any given way. Normally, pitchers can dictate the game when they're on. But pitchers can't dictate to him. And this is just a normal year for him."

It may be more than that, actually. In Japan, where the season lasts 130 games, Ichiro had just one 200-hit season.

"He was supposed to come over and need some time to adjust," Mark McLemore said. "I guess he got his adjustment period out of the way on the flight over."

– John Hickey

PARADE

How Ichiro surpassed 'Shoeless Joe' Jackson as the most prolific rookie hitter in baseball hi

April	May	June	July	August	September
39	47	38	30	51	30
336	379	339	268	429	337

BRET BOONE
The year's big surprise turns on the power

WHAT COULD BE said clearly about the season, following the Mariners' fifth series sweep of the season back in May, was that it was preposterous.

Rather than slowing down after a hot April, the Mariners got better.

In winning eight games in a row, the Mariners averaged seven runs a game.

In that same streak, they invented an All-Star second baseman out of a journeyman.

"I've never been on a team like this," said the invention in question, Bret Boone, who played on the 1999 Atlanta Braves team that won 103 games and reached the World Series.

The distinction?

"We just find so many ways to win," Boone said. "We come to the ballpark expecting to win."

The Mariners' style this season was to flick fingers incessantly behind the opponents' ears, as opposed to a direct punch in the nose. That doesn't explain Boone, who finished with 37 home runs. Then again, nothing explains Boone, who at .331, hit 76 points over his career average.

In that eight-game winning streak in May, Boone hit .420. In the field, he made only a single error in the season's first 40 games. This from a 32-year-old journeyman on a one-year contract, playing with his fourth team in four seasons.

As much a revelation as was Ichiro, Boone was nearly the full lineup replacement, qualitatively as well as quantitatively, for Alex Rodriguez.

"It's about the right time (in his career) for him to come together, physically and mentally," manag-er Lou Piniella said. "He's matured a lot as a play-er. He's tempered his cockiness a bit. He's more selective than when we had him before. He's learned the strike zone, and he puts the ball in play.

"And he's a really solid, solid second baseman."

Often a dead-pull hacker in his first go-round in Seattle (1992-93), Boone now patiently uses the entire field. He spent considerable time before the season with his father, Cincinnati manager Bob Boone, altering his batting approach to get more from his lower body and less from his hands.

"In the big picture, I'm still a free swinger," Boone said in assessing his torrid start. "But from the beginning of this season, I've had good at-bats when I've needed them. I really like hitting with runners on base. From an RBI standpoint, I started clicking last year, then I got hurt" when a knee injury in San Diego limited him to 127 games.

"I feel like I can keep going at this pace – well, not quite, or I'd drive in 160 runs."

Boone came close, finishing with 141 RBIs. Every baseball team that unexpectedly bolts ahead of the field has at least one player who blows the doors off his career norms. Boone was the Mariners' pattern-breaker.

"I'm sick of hitting 20 homers and .260," he said back in May. "I think I can get 25 homers and hit .290 or .300. I want to get up there."

The laws of baseball averages may have suggest-ed otherwise. But those laws had a bad several months in Seattle.

– Art Thiel

Bret Boone was known more for defense than offense when he rejoined the Mariners in 2001. He changed all that and revived a seldom-heard phrase – slugging second baseman. PHOTOGRAPH BY MIKE URBAN

SECOND TO NONE

THIRTY-SIX HOME RUNS. These days, it doesn't sound all that impressive. After all, Mark McGwire and Barry Bonds can put 36 in the rear view mirror by June.

But try this for perspective: American League teams have combined to play 996 seasons in the past century, and in none of them did a second baseman hit more home runs than Bret Boone did this season – 36, plus one as a designated hitter.

Many legendary second basemen never came close to 36. Joe Morgan never hit more than 27. Charlie Gehringer topped out at 20. Craig Biggio, 22. Bobby Grich, 30. Bill Mazeroski, 19.

A 5-foot-10, 190-pounder who never had hit more than 24 in a season, Boone suddenly is a record-setting power hitter.

Traditionally, down the spine of the field – catcher, second base, shortstop and center field – teams accept lesser hitters in favor of outstanding defensive players.

Though there always have been exceptions, in the past 15 years, more and more players have broken through at those positions with good defense as well as offensive skill. Cal Ripken ushered in the era of the big shortstop, and Alex Rodriguez and Nomar Garciaparra are among the best hitters in the game.

So do Boone, also an outstanding defensive player, and San Francisco's Jeff Kent usher in the era of the slugging second baseman?

"It's never going to be like first base or DH or left field, but look at what the shortstops have done," said Boone, who played shortstop as an amateur, including his career at USC. "The shortstops were virtually never power guys, with the rare exception of Cal and Ernie Banks."

With a .331 batting average, Boone became the first AL second baseman with 30 home runs and a .300-plus average. With 141 RBIs, he overtook Gehringer for the AL second-base mark. He fell six home runs short of the major league mark of 42, set by Rogers Hornsby in 1922.

"It's a great record. I'm proud of it," he said of the AL home-run mark. "It wasn't the first thing on my list; I mean, I want a ring. But if I said the individual things are no big deal, I'd be lying.

"I did something no one else has ever done before, and I'm proud to have done it."

– David Andriesen

> "BOONIE'S BEEN OUR LEADER ALL YEAR. HE'S A REAL PROFESSIONAL HITTER."
> – Lou Piniella

Boone watches his record-tying 33rd home run clear the outfield wall. He hit more home runs and drove in more runs than any other second baseman in American League history.

PHOTOGRAPH BY MIKE URBAN

THIS GUY PRODUCES

Ichiro is a phenomenon, a delightful gift from Japanese baseball who placed the collective jaw of American baseball on its collective puffy chest with remarkable skills at bat and in the field.

But the American League's Most Valuable Player? No.

Not quite. A viable candidate, certainly. But second on his own team to Bret Boone.

Much as the highest value in real estate is location, the highest value in baseball is run production. And Boone is the AL's best.

Boone has made the biggest contribution for the best team. Emotion and entertainment aside, Boone's work is slightly more important than Ichiro's because without him, Ichiro simply doesn't get home nearly as often, no matter how many infield hits and stolen bases he accumulates.

Ichiro has had nothing less than an astonishing first year in the majors. If points were awarded for exotica, he would deserve not only the MVP but his own cable show and cologne. But baseball awards tend to gravitate toward the ordinary and traditional, such as runs.

The one most responsible for the runs that made the Mariners extraordinary and untraditional is the squatty guy at second base.

– Art Thiel

Boone, here hugging teammate John Olerud, had plenty to celebrate this season.

PHOTOGRAPH BY MIKE URBAN

FREDDY GARCIA
An ace comes of age on a Fenway night

IN BOSTON, THEY are used to this kind of pitching as the drive toward the postseason intensifies.

They just aren't used to this kind of quiet.

Freddy Garcia came into sold-out Fenway Park last night and did a Pedro Martinez impersonation. The Mariners starter dominated the Red Sox from the first pitch in Seattle's 6-2 victory.

Martinez has been doing this for the Sox for years. The crowds have uniformly screamed their lungs out for him. They can't this month, because Martinez is spending his August on the disabled list.

Garcia isn't Pedro, but he's not bad. Garcia pitched eight innings, allowed three hits, walked two and never let the Sox or their fans think they were in the game.

And with Edgar Martinez contributing his second three-run homer in as many nights, the Mariners were able to reinforce the feeling of futility that seemed to grip Fenway.

"I like it loud," Garcia said, harkening back to winter ball in his native Venezuela, where games are never quiet. "I like the people excited. But if I make them quiet, that's a good feeling."

The only moment of good cheer for Boston came in the bottom of the first. A walk and a single set up Manny Ramirez's RBI grounder, tying the game at 1. By the time the Sox got their next baserunner, Seattle had a 5-1 lead. It was never in doubt the rest of the way.

"This was a little like playoff ball," Garcia said. "Last night especially. They were loud. But tonight they weren't so loud."

What was loud was Garcia's overhand curve. It's a pitch most right-handed pitchers don't throw, particularly from Garcia's release point, directly over his head. Most pitchers throw sidearm. That makes Garcia's curve special.

"That's got to be difficult, hitting against that," fellow starter Paul Abbott said. "He's 6-foot-5, and he really gets his arm up there over his head. The pitch comes at you hard, then it breaks fast. It's something special to watch."

Martinez, whose three-run blast in the third was followed by a Bret Boone solo shot, is just as happy not to have to face Garcia.

"It's one thing when a hard thrower like that starts you out with a fastball," Martinez said. "You have a pretty good idea of what might be coming (next). But when he breaks that big curveball down on you for a strike, I'll guarantee you the hitter doesn't know what's coming next."

It could be another curve. Or a 96-mph fastball. Or a changeup, a pitch that Garcia masks. It looks like he's going to pop a fastball, but the pitch comes in about 78 mph. Hitters can screw themselves into the ground trying to adjust mid-swing.

Garcia had streaks where he retired six, five and eight batters in succession. After the first inning, only a Trot Nixon triple caused him trouble. Again it was a ground ball that got the run in for Boston in the sixth. The Red Sox didn't get another hit as Garcia and Arthur Rhodes put the Sox away for Seattle's 87th victory.

The Mariners are 54 games over .500. They suffered their most devastating loss of the season just over a week ago, when they blew a 12-run lead in Cleveland. Since then, however, they've won seven of nine games.

"We play hard every day," Garcia said. "We don't quit."

— John Hickey

"HE'S GOT GREAT STUFF, AN ABOVE-AVERAGE FASTBALL, PRETTY DARN GOOD CURVEBALL AND A CHANGEUP OR SPLITTER. AND HE MIXES IT UP. HE'S PRETTY TOUGH."
– Anaheim outfielder
Tim Salmon

A power pitcher with finesse, Freddy Garcia had a career-high 18 victories and led all American League starters with an earned-run average of 3.05. PHOTOGRAPH BY PAUL KITAGAKI JR.

JAMIE MOYER
Success comes with hard work and a soft touch

JAMIE MOYER WILL be on the mound for the Mariners this afternoon.

Should be a couch.

If not that, a recliner.

Something prone.

Most guys his age – 38 – would be flipping channels, considering a nap, wasting away a Saturday afternoon.

Not Moyer. To hear him talk, he's merely at the halfway point of a 30-year, big-league career.

Retirement plans? Are you kidding?

"With everything being in line and being healthy, I'd love to pitch in my 40s," the lefty said. "I'd love to end my career here at 42, 43, 46, 54. OK, that's getting carried away a little."

To know Moyer, maybe not.

He continues to show up each year an unchanged man, winning more than his share of games, defying all gravitational pulls that rearrange the baseball atmosphere each year.

Against Minnesota today, Moyer will make his 21st start this season, trying to build on a 10-5 record. The Twins can expect a pillow fight.

Moyer has built his career on the changeup, once claiming he could throw the pitch at 14 different speeds. Not only are his offerings deathly slow, they rarely miss the target. He has walked just 27 batters in 121 innings and thrown just one wild pitch.

Therein lies his fountain of youth.

"When he's done, it will be because he loses his control," Mariners second baseman Bret Boone said.

Boone doubts he'll still be a big-leaguer at 38. So does fellow Mariners pitcher Aaron Sele. "That would put me at another eight years," the right-hander said. "Is it conceivable? I would say no."

Eyeing his ageless teammate, Sele reconsidered. "The best thing I've got going for me is watching him, the way he takes care of himself, the way he works at it," Sele said.

Acquired in a 1996 trade from Boston, Moyer has seen his career flourish with the Mariners, resulting in 6-2, 17-5, 15-9, 14-8 and 13-10 seasons. Besides his obvious pitching skills, he credited tireless conditioning for increasing his baseball life span.

Before every game except the one in which he pitched, Moyer ran in the outfield. Often, he was the only player. Sprints, jogs, laps. Home and away. Fitness meant victories. Expended sweat meant extended years.

A not-so-funny thing happened this season – he doesn't run anymore. At least not the way he would like.

Moyer's season ended last year during the playoffs, in a simulated game, when a liner struck his left kneecap, fracturing it.

The pitcher showed up for spring training and it hurt to run. He tried again in April. More discomfort. Unnerved momentarily, Moyer found another, less appealing outlet. He rides a stationary bike. Eighteen minutes per day. Every day. Mix in the usual weightlifting with a few trips to Safeco Field's compact swimming pool, and the pitcher has maintained his svelte physique, kept his endurance levels up.

Moyer didn't pitch well near the end of last season, and some pressbox observers concluded he was done, that youngsters would be circling his spot like vultures.

Instead, he has been his usual, steady self, enjoying this season as much as any since he first broke into the majors with the 1986 Cubs. With solid relief and defense behind him, Moyer has even allowed himself to envision every starter's dream.

"I would love to win 20 games," he said. "I've never done that."

– **Dan Raley**

"HE THROWS A LOT OF INNINGS. HE HAS A GREAT HITS-TO-INNINGS RATIO. HE'S EVERYTHING YOU WANT."
– Mariners pitching coach Bryan Price

Jamie Moyer baffled hitters again and made a dream come true: He became a 20-game winner. PHOTOGRAPH BY DAN DeLONG

EDGAR MARTINEZ
Humble DH strengthens his hold on Seattle's heart

"HAS THERE EVER BEEN A MORE BELOVED MARINER THAN EDGAR? I DON'T THINK SO."
– Dave Niehaus

THE E-MAIL was smoking.

"Yo, I don't know what game you were watching, but it wasn't Ichiro who sparked the comeback win for the Mariners in their opener. It was Edgar Martinez! If he doesn't get three hits and drive in a run, the Mariners lose."

The voicemail was blistering:

"Fine. Ichiro had a couple of hits and scored a run. Nice story. I'm happy for the guy. I'm happy for Japan. But the heart and soul of this team is Edgar. Wake up!"

Consider me awake.

Starting the day with reminders that Martinez is the most beloved, important and enduring Mariner is welcome, especially in light of the team's inspired start.

Last night, in the Mariners' second game, it was Martinez, not Ichiro, who received the loudest ovation when he stepped to the plate. And when Oakland starter Barry Zito threw inside to Martinez, nearly hitting him, the boos were deafening. You could almost imagine an incensed mob storming the mound to defend his honor.

Certainly, Ichiro's historic debut deserved a lot of ink. But just as certain, the preponderance of Ichiromania surrounding the team's opener followed a familiar pattern when it comes to Martinez.

It's not that Martinez is a low-profile player. Not with the best batting average (.324) of any designated hitter in history, not with two American League batting titles, and not after smacking 37 homers – a career best – last season, when he led the league with 145 runs batted in.

It's just that nice, quiet people who shy away from star treatment tend to go on the back burner, behind the Big Units and Juniors and A-Rods. But now, fans are adamant that Ichiro not eclipse their beloved Edgar.

"He isn't your typical superstar," second baseman Bret Boone said. "His attitude won't tell you that, but his stats say he is. Sometimes, you tell him how much you like to watch him hit, it's like he's embarrassed. In today's game, once you get to a certain level, it's like you're expected to act different. Edgar doesn't follow that way."

It almost hurts to bring up the subject of salaries in regard to Martinez, because he has been the anti-star in this category as well. In April, a deal was struck that made him the highest-paid Mariner ever when his contract was extended through 2002, with a club option for 2003.

After years of being relegated to secondary status behind the Big Three, the new deal – $9 million for 2002 – was a statement not just by the Mariners. It was a statement by Martinez.

After deliberating all winter, Martinez approached the Mariners during spring training, telling the team he was not ready to retire.

"He came to us and indicated he was in great physical shape. He wanted to play a couple more seasons after this season, would we entertain an extension?" Mariners CEO Howard Lincoln said. After negotiating with Scott Boras and A-Rod, an extension for Martinez was "like a sea change. It was gentlemanly. It was a pleasure," Lincoln said.

In theory, $9 million is steep for a designated hitter who will be 39 next year. Lincoln did not refer to market value, but to Mariner value.

"You look at that footage from the '95 series against the Yankees, and everyone talks about Griffey rounding the bases. I'm not taking anything away from Ken, but who the hell hit that ball? That was Edgar's double that won the game. He has done that repeatedly over the years."

– **Laura Vecsey**

Edgar Martinez kept his sweet stroke at age 38, hitting better than .300 for the 10th time. PHOTOGRAPH BY GILBERT W. ARIAS

Martinez gets high fives from Carlos Guillen after hitting a grand slam against the Chicago White Sox.

PHOTOGRAPH BY
GILBERT W. ARIAS

MAN OF THE PEOPLE

VETERANS DAY WAS celebrated last night at Safeco Field.

Jamie Moyer, 38, won his first complete game since 1999. Edgar Martinez, also 38, singled home one run, then homered for his 1,000th career run batted in.

Martinez's homer bounced off the electronic scoreboard in left field. By the time he made his tour of the bases, accepted congratulations from teammates and tried to settle on the bench, he found himself prodded to take a curtain call.

The milestone is a sign of longevity and performance. The crowd of 45,450 wouldn't sit until it could show its appreciation.

"At first, I wasn't sure I was going to come out," Martinez said.

With the clamor increasing and teammates egging him on, Martinez ultimately climbed to the second step of the dugout, took off his batting helmet and waved it a couple of times. Only then did he return to his seat, another job well done.

"That meant a lot to me after playing all these years here," Martinez said. "It's a great level to get to. It's felt good to play all this time with one team. And to have the fans do what they did was special."

Ichiro said the Mariners savored the moment along with Martinez.

"To get to 1,000 is special; that's 100 RBIs a year for 10 years," Ichiro said. "And then when the fans respond to him the way they do, it's great. He's a franchise guy. The people love him."

– John Hickey

HOLI, CAN
EDGAR TAKE
ME TO THE
PROM?
- A teen-age
girl's plea to
Martinez's
wife, on a sign
at Safeco
Field

Breaking bats and records, Martinez has earned his billing as baseball's best designated hitter.

PHOTOGRAPH BY
DAN DeLONG

THE SEASON

APRIL
Mariners make a statement, and so does Ichiro

OAKLAND (APRIL 11) – The Mariners keep throwing pitchers at the Athletics.

Tonight, they threw pitchers and a right fielder.

In both cases, it was no contest.

Aaron Sele churned out a henhouse full of eggs, throwing eight zeroes in the Mariners' 3-0 victory over the A's.

And in the one scant moment that Sele's mastery of the moment seemed in doubt, Ichiro Suzuki came up with a throw from right field that needs to be framed and hung on the wall at the Louvre next to the Mona Lisa.

It was that much a thing of beauty.

In the bottom of the eighth inning, with the swift Terrence Long running from first base, Ichiro fielded Ramon Hernandez's grounder and threw an eye-high laser to third base. Long should have been in easily. Against another arm, anyway. Against Ichiro, he never had a chance.

Long slid into third base to find David Bell clutching the ball and making the tag.

Sele finished the inning having allowed just four hits and one walk in the 103 pitches he scattered over eight innings. It was the most dominating pitching performance of the season for the Mariners. And yet, when the game was over, all anyone wanted to talk about was the throw.

Make that The Throw.

– John Hickey

SEATTLE (APRIL 16) – Before tonight's game, Alex Rodriguez tried to defuse bitterness with one of the most politically correct press conferences in Seattle history.

In the distant and recent past, Rodriguez was a man accused of saying all the wrong things, about the Mariners not being a factor in the negotiations and telling Boeing it should saddle up with him in Big D.

But there he was, praising Seattle, praising the Mariners, praising the fans. If he had gone on much longer, he probably would have praised the rain.

Hyperbole extended to the Mariners, Rodriguez offering the flattering but implausible forecast of his former team winning 110 to 115 games this season.

"They have the complete package," he said.

– Jim Moore

SEATTLE (APRIL 22) – You want a hot start? The 1981 Oakland Athletics began the year 18-1.

For 19 games, the Mariners can't match that.

But for 19 games in 2001, no one in the American League West comes close to matching the Mariners.

Seattle's 5-0 victory over Anaheim today completed a 15-4 rumble through the West. The Mariners are 11 games over .500. Texas, 5 1/2 games back in second place, has as many losses as victories.

What does it all mean? Perhaps not as much as one might think. The numbers are impressive, but the Mariners are less than 12 percent of the way through the season. The Mariners have demonstrated they can win; they have yet to prove they can win over a full season.

But for now, the Mariners are doing everything well. The starting pitchers yielded three runs in 25

Bret Boone epitomized the Mariners offense – much bigger than advertised. PHOTOGRAPH BY MIKE URBAN

Seattle's Opening Night pitcher, Freddy Garcia got stronger as the season progressed.

PHOTOGRAPH BY
GILBERT W. ARIAS

innings in the four-game sweep of Anaheim. The defense continues to dazzle. The hitters keep grinding out the four, five or six runs it takes to support that pitching.

"It's a good start. It means we're doing what we need to do to win," pitcher Aaron Sele said. "We're making the most of our opportunities. But 15-4 also means it's early. We need to stretch this out over 162 games."

It's not that Sele and mates expect to win 15 of every 19 games. That would produce 128 victories, most in major league history.

– John Hickey

NEW YORK (APRIL 25) – The temperature fell 18 degrees here today.

After a glimpse of spring yesterday, long sleeves, long pants and long coats were once again the order of the day.

So were long faces on Yankees fans. It turns out a cooling off at Yankee Stadium could do little to cool off the Mariners.

Credit Carlos Guillen, who came up with two huge, two-out hits for the Mariners. The second, a sixth-inning RBI single, came just moments after the Yankees had scored three runs to tie the score at 5. Guillen gave the Mariners the lead. On the next pitch, Ichiro made it 7-5 with an RBI single.

That's the way it ended, after the Mariners bullpen shackled the world champions. Only one Yankee reached base in the final three innings as the Mariners won their sixth in a row and improved their record to 17-4, the best in baseball.

Guillen initiated the scoring in the series opener with a bases-loaded, two-run single off Roger Clemens in the second inning. The Mariners won 7-5.

He duplicated the feat tonight with a bases-loaded, two-run single off Andy Pettitte, also in the second inning. And the Mariners won 7-5 again. As Yogi Berra once said, it was déjà vu all over again.

"We don't need Alex Rodriguez," reliever Arthur Rhodes said in reference to the shortstop Guillen replaced. "We've got a pretty good shortstop here."

– John Hickey

"PEOPLE TALK ABOUT POWER. BUT WHEN YOU GET PITCHING AND SCORE A FEW RUNS, YOU DON'T NEED POWER. YOU DON'T. THIS IS WINNING BASEBALL."
– Arthur Rhodes

THE SEASON AT A GLANCE

APRIL

2
The Mariners rally from a 4-0 deficit on Opening Night to defeat Oakland before a record crowd at Safeco Field.

11
Alex Rodriguez goes 1 for 5 in his return to Seattle. The Mariners improve to 10-3 with a 9-7 victory over the Rangers.

Former Mariners superstar Alex Rodriguez shares a laugh with the team's dazzling newcomer, Ichiro Suzuki.

PHOTOGRAPH BY
PAUL KITAGAKI JR.

Fans at Safeco Field were not amused, booing Rodriguez and holding money to signify the $252 million contract he signed with Texas.

PHOTOGRAPH BY
PAUL KITAGAKI JR.

13
The Mariners win 7-3 at Oakland, sweeping the Athletics in a three-game series for the first time since 1993.

26
The Mariners complete a three-game sweep at Yankee Stadium, defeating Roger Clemens, Andy Pettitte and Mike Mussina on consecutive days.

28
The Mariners soar to 20-4 with their ninth consecutive victory, 8-5 over the White Sox in Chicago. They finish the month with a major league record 20 victories and a nine-game lead in the AL West.

MAY
It gets even better for the hottest team in baseball

"EDGAR'S JUST A NIGHTMARE."
– Minnesota manager Tom Kelly on pitching to Edgar Martinez. The Mariners DH had 25 RBIs in May.

SEATTLE (MAY 2) – Tonight was the first U.S. meeting between Hideo Nomo and Ichiro Suzuki, but not their first meeting. Nomo struck out Ichiro the first time they met in Japan's Pacific League in 1993, then Ichiro hit his first major-league home run off Nomo. Ichiro had a .308 career average against Nomo in Japan, well below his overall average of .353. They last faced each other in the fall of 1996.

"I don't think we are bad friends," Nomo said, "but it's kind of hard to say we're good buddies."

Akio Hayano of Japan's NHK television network said the two were very competitive: "They were like rivals, enemies." If they weren't enemies before, they might be now.

After Ichiro grounded out and flied out in his first two at-bats tonight, he took a 90-mph Nomo fastball between the shoulder blades in the fifth inning.

You could almost hear the tabloid presses in Japan revving to double speed.

– David Andriesen

SEATTLE (MAY 3) – If baseball is all about pitching, pitching is all about walks.

Or, more properly stated, lack of walks.

In an age where the statisticians' mantra is "on-base percentage," the pitcher can take that percentage and grind it into dust by throwing strikes and avoiding walks.

Sounds simple. It isn't, or everyone would do it.

Going all out, Mark McLemore demonstrates Seattle's speed on the basepaths. PHOTOGRAPH BY PAUL KITAGAKI JR.

MAY

2
Aaron Sele pitches seven strong innings, stopping the Mariners' first two-game losing streak in a 5-1 win over Boston.

9
The Mariners score five runs with two outs in the eighth inning to defeat Boston 10-5 at Fenway Park.

10
Kazuhiro Sasaki records his 16th save and the Mariners beat Boston 5-2 to win another road series.

Tonight at Safeco Field, Jamie Moyer was just the latest Mariner to dabble in the craft. He allowed one walk in seven innings, making the Red Sox earn their way on base.

The Sox didn't have it in them to hit that much. Sure, they totaled 11 hits, but only one was of significance in a 10-3 Seattle victory.

The real significance tonight was that the Mariners came back from losing Tuesday to win games two and three and take the series. It's the ninth consecutive series win for the Mariners to start the season.

– John Hickey

SEATTLE (MAY 17) – Before today's game, David Wells asked Ichiro Suzuki for one of his bats, complete with an autograph.

Such is the interest in Ichiro these days. Even the opposing pitcher wants a memento.

Chicago's Wells would have been better served by sending an emissary into the Mariners' clubhouse to pilfer all of Ichiro's bats.

The one Ichiro had left was plenty good enough to handle Wells. Ichiro went 2-for-4 against Wells and added a single off reliever Jon Garland to help the Mariners win 5-1 and sweep the White Sox.

Ichiro makes a diving catch of a drive by Baltimore's Brady Anderson. Fans called right field "Area 51" because balls hit there usually disappeared – into Ichiro's glove.

PHOTOGRAPH BY
PAUL KITAGAKI JR.

Ichiro's 22-game hitting streak, the longest in the major leagues this year, is one short of Ichiro's professional best – he had two 23-game streaks in Japan. He is two shy of Joey Cora's 1997 club record.

Today, Ichiro singled up the middle in his first at-bat, stole second and third, then scored on an Edgar Martinez single to put Wells in an immediate 1-0 hole. Wells and White Sox never recovered.

– John Hickey

KANSAS CITY (MAY 28) – In one sense, the Kansas City Royals pounded the Mariners this holiday weekend, hitting twice as many homers as the Mariners.

The outhomered Mariners were not, however, outgunned. Seattle won all four games against Kansas City, completing the sweep with a 13-3 victory today.

The Seattle style of 2001 would have played well in 1901. And in their bid to compensate for a perceived lack of power, the Mariners are perhaps redefining the way baseball should be played in the new century.

They hit. They walk. They run. They score. Their pitching does the rest. Kansas City's six homers in the four-game series produced seven runs. Total. Seattle answered by averaging 8½ runs per game, even though the Mariners hit only three home runs.

In this age of power baseball, the Mariners are 10th in the American League in home runs. Yet they are first in the majors in wins, and 25 games over .500 for the first time in club history.

– John Hickey

With a 23-game hitting streak, Ichiro was named American League rookie of the month – again.

PHOTOGRAPH BY
PAUL KITAGAKI JR.

SEATTLE (MAY 31) – Aaron Sele, dismissed by the Orioles two winters ago as injured and not worth the dispersal of valuable free-agent money, eked out a measure of revenge tonight by recording his 100th career win in the Mariners' 2-1 victory over Baltimore.

Not that he would admit to that satisfaction.

"It's not something I think about a lot," said Sele, who agreed to a four-year contract with the Orioles after the 1999 season. Before the contract was signed, Orioles owner Peter Angelos squirmed out of the commitment with the claim that Sele's elbow was injured.

Some injury. Sele is 8-0 this season, 25-10 since joining the Mariners and the second-winningest pitcher in baseball since the start of the 1998 season. Pedro Martinez of the Red Sox has 67 wins over the span. Sele has won 62 times, putting him in elite company.

Sele has made 11 starts this season, and the Mariners are 11-0 in those games. His 2.65 earned-run average is second among American League starters. He's walked 11 men in 11 starts. When he walked two batters in the first inning, jaws dropped.

He hadn't walked two men in an inning all season.

– John Hickey

JUNE
The lead gets wider, with Boone the big bopper

SEATTLE (JUNE 8) – You thought they were just stretching.

A few hours before the first pitch, the Mariners congregate in right field. Like little boys, they flop down in the grass. They twist and turn. They tell stories, trade insults.

They dream.

"They show the division standings on the scoreboard and ours comes up last," pitcher Paul Abbott said. "I pay attention. I want to see it. It doesn't come around like this every 100 years. It's like Halley's comet. It doesn't look right."

Today, as the Mariners loosen up for a three-game series with the San Diego Padres, the following will flicker across Safeco Field's rectangular, electronic wall:

Seattle, 46-12, .793, 17½ games ahead.

Yesterday, the Mariners put their bats and balls away for 24 hours. In unison, the rest of the American League West shouted thank you. Lately, an off day is the only way to keep the home club from the win column.

Just one big-league team has started faster than the Mariners – the 1912 New York Giants had one more victory, one less loss. Only two other teams have maintained the Mariners' pace – the 1907 Chicago Cubs and 1939 New York Yankees.

Before, you could argue this was merely a statistical aberration. But now, we're in June. What if it's not?

– Dan Raley

Second baseman Bret Boone brought slick fielding to Seattle, along with his big bat.

PHOTOGRAPH BY MIKE URBAN

SEATTLE (JUNE 10) – Today was Two-Headed Calf Day at the ballpark.

Ichiro showed off his home-run trot.

John Halama pitched seven shutout innings.

Weirdest of all, Al Martin had two hits.

These signs can only mean the Mariners are back to putting their pants on two legs at a time.

After a one-game sojourn to the loss column yesterday, causing quarrelsome digestion among the masses, distemper among pets and a 5.0 earthquake, the Mariners circus is back in full freak.

The calliope played loudest for Martin, who in the 8-1 victory over the San Diego Padres had a double and a two-run home run – only the third time in his agonizing, 79-game Seattle tenure that he's had two extra-base hits.

Hitting has been so bad for Martin that Jay Buhner put his teammate's bats in the clubhouse sauna, in an attempt to heat them up. Lately Martin has adopted the custom of Bret Boone, making the rice balls prepared by Ichiro's bride a staple of his diet.

But the going got weirdest when Martin was given the bats of Aaron Sele, who has a reputation as perhaps the worst hitting pitcher in the major leagues.

"I was thinking," Martin said, smiling, "two negatives might make a positive."

– Art Thiel

OAKLAND (JUNE 21) – Not that there's a big demand for it, but if you want to know how much unexpected fun can be had in a four-day tooth pull, replay tapes of the Mariners' series against the Oakland A's that ended in a 2-2 drop-deadlock.

"This," said Mariners second baseman Bret Boone, "was a very good series – they were ahead, we were ahead, lots of long innings and everything coming down to the last at-bat."

That summarized the Mariners' 12-10 victory today, as well as the 6-4 defeat the night before, the 8-7 win before that and the 4-3 loss before that.

For an allegedly dead team, the A's fogged a lot of mirrors this week. For an allegedly world-beating team, the Mariners were thrilled, exhausted and semi-amazed to come out of the Coliseum with a split.

Today's rollicking festival of wood was the ultimate example. Even the quiet moments were high entertainment. With two outs and nobody on in the fifth inning, manager Lou Piniella ordered A's slugger Jason Giambi walked intentionally.

What the moved lacked in manhood, it made up for in strategy. Giambi already had a double and a home run, and the next batter, the .133-hitting John Jaha, grounded weakly to short.

"First time I've ever done that," said Piniella, smiling wanly as he thought about the earlier fraternal homers by Jason and Jeremy. "I had enough of the Giambis today."

As he was talking, Piniella was on his second postgame cigarette and fumbling for a third. After today, nobody would have blamed him if he were screaming to know who threw his potted plant overboard.

As it was, much of his pitching staff is temporarily out to sea.

For the series, the Mariners bullpen gave up 10

Freddy Garcia earns cheers at Safeco Field, moving closer to his first All-Star berth.
PHOTOGRAPH BY PAUL KITAGAKI JR.

earned runs in 12 2/3 innings. The starter today, John Halama, gave up six runs in the first.

Most any other team would be dead from cuts. The Mariners were just putting on the boxing gloves.

They whaled back with two runs in the second, three in the third, one in the fourth and three in the fifth. After taking rounds six and seven off to rope-a-dope, they pounded two in the eighth and one in the ninth.

In a word – astonishing.

– Art Thiel

SEATTLE (JUNE 24) – Teammate Al Martin playfully calls him Thurston Howell III because Bret Boone reminds him of the conceited million-aire played by Jim Backus on "Gilligan's Island."

"He thinks he's better than everybody else, even when he's going bad," Martin said. "But now he *is* better than everybody else."

Today in a 7-3 victory over Anaheim at Safeco Field, Boone continued his torrid season, stroking an RBI single and a solo homer to raise his batting average to .324.

The shortest Mariner (listed at 5-foot-10) hit his 20th homer and drove in his 78th run, more RBIs than any Mariners second baseman has produced in one season. Boone still has 88 games remaining.

David Bell, who now plays third base, had 20 homers and 77 RBIs in 1999.

Boone's next home run will be a club record for second basemen.

"It's been a good month so far," said Boone, who has 10 home runs and 28 RBIs in June and is hitting .455 against left-handed pitchers.

Whether coincidental or not, the 32-year-old dyed his hair about a month ago, adding blonde highlights.

"He's been hitting well since he got that 'N Sync haircut," said reliever Norm Charlton. "Right now there's no way to get him out. He's hitting balls above his head and hitting balls off his shoe tops, and hitting 'em out."

– Jim Moore

JULY
Garcia sparkles during All-Star month

LOS ANGELES (JULY 6) – They came to see Ichiro.

Those who stuck around saw a sterling effort from another of the Northwest's stars.

Freddy Garcia, who shut out Anaheim five days ago, took a no-hitter into the sixth inning tonight in front of a sellout crowd at Dodger Stadium.

He lost the no-hitter but very little else. Garcia finished with a four-hit shutout, his second in succession, and a 13-0 victory that gets him to the All-Star break with a 10-1 record and a 3.18 earned-run average.

The next game will be Tuesday's All-Star Game. No pitcher goes into the game on more of a roll than Garcia, who has thrown 18 consecutive scoreless innings, allowing just 12 hits.

Ichiro was the early focus of the crowd. Camera flashes went off with every pitch to him, much in the way they did when Mark McGwire and Sammy Sosa were engaged in their epic home run chase in 1998.

Ichiro didn't disappoint. He homered in his first at-bat, singled twice, walked and scored two runs. The home run off Kevin Brown was a monster, a 400-plus footer that landed in the right-field bleachers, halfway up.

"That was an awesome way to start," Garcia said. "That was a beautiful way to start the game."

– John Hickey

CONTINUED ON PAGE 68

University of Washington students Leanne Tanizawa and Carolyn Sueno pose for the camera through a cardboard cutout at All-Star FanFest, a participatory event that set the stage for the big game.

PHOTOGRAPH BY MERYL SCHENKER

SEATTLE SHOWCASE

Eight Mariners add luster to Cal Ripken's shining night

JULY 10 – It has worked for the Mariners all season. It worked for the American League All-Stars tonight.

Ichiro Suzuki got the game rolling, and Kazuhiro Sasaki wrapped it up.

In between Ichiro's leadoff hit and Sasaki's easy save, Seattle's six other All-Stars contributed to the AL's 4-1 victory over the National League. Right-hander Freddy Garcia earned the win, Sasaki recorded the save and Mike Cameron stretched a single into a double with sheer hustle.

Mostly, however, Seattle players reveled in the overwhelming support shown by the sellout Safeco Field crowd every time one of them stepped into the batter's box or trotted in from the bullpen. A banner high above the center-field bleachers read "Home of the Great Seattle Eight" and no one could argue that tonight.

It was only fitting for the game's leading vote-getter that Ichiro led off the first inning with a hit off former Mariners star Randy Johnson. First baseman Todd Helton made a diving stop on Ichiro's sharply hit line drive, but his throw to Johnson at first was too late for the out. Moments later, Ichiro stole second base for good measure.

That turned out to be the only hit Johnson surrendered in two innings, and Ichiro's only time on base. Ichiro was humble about the matchup, and seemed genuinely moved by the adulation he received from fans and All-Stars alike.

"I'm very honored just to face Randy Johnson in an All-Star Game," said Ichiro, who grounded out to second base and third base in his other at-bats. "Whether I got a hit off him or not, he is a great pitcher. He wore the number 51 before me as a Mariner, and I always keep in my mind to keep the number 51 with dignity, since I inherited it from Randy."

The other Seattle players seemed to save that kind of reverence for the game itself – whether they affected the outcome or not.

Garcia got the win with a seven-pitch effort in a scoreless third. Sasaki retired the side in the ninth. After striking out the Reds' Sean Casey, he got the Marlins' Cliff Floyd on a ground ball to first for the final out.

Mariners second baseman Bret Boone was 0-for-2 as the cleanup hitter. Designated hitter Edgar Martinez also was hitless. First baseman John Olerud reached base on a throwing error.

That didn't mean they enjoyed the experience any less.

"I think it was great for what's going on in the city this year, for how well we've done in the first half," Boone said. "What epitomized it was to see the look on Mike Cameron's face, and how excited he was."

F-18 jets from Whidbey Island Naval Air Station roar over pregame ceremonies at a packed Safeco Field.

PHOTOGRAPH BY PAUL KITAGAKI JR.

You'd be hard-pressed to find anyone more determined to bask in the experience than Cameron, who was named to the All-Star team Sunday. When the second-year Mariner wasn't taking batting practice, he was sitting in the AL dugout – cap turned backward, mouth turned upward in a broad smile – taking in the sights and sounds.

When he got the chance to participate, he made it count, stretching his sixth-inning single into a double – never looking for anything less.

"It was an adrenaline thing. He had no chance to stop me, because I was too excited," Cameron said. "This was definitely as exciting as I ever thought it would be."

– Holly Cain

Mariners closer Kazuhiro Sasaki celebrates with teammates after saving the American League's victory.

PHOTOGRAPH BY PAUL KITAGAKI JR.

Cal Ripken Jr. holds his Most Valuable Player award. It was the final All-Star appearance for Ripken, who retired after 21 years with Baltimore.

PHOTOGRAPH BY DAN DeLONG

CAL WORKS HIS MAGIC

JULY 10 – On the first pitch to him in the third inning of his 18th and final All-Star Game, Cal Ripken hit a home run.

Curtain down. Lights up. G'night, everybody.

He won the Most Valuable Player award, the commissioner's Historic Achievement award, a Boy Scout brag rag and the Martha Stewart Pinch-Cheek-And-Say-"Wudgie-Wudgie" trophy.

The temptation is to say that National League pitcher Chan Ho Park must have grooved the pitch. But that doesn't take into consideration the fact that Ripken homered in his next-to-last at-bat during his previous visit to Seattle on May 31.

He now has more homers this year in Seattle than Alex Rodriguez. And Ripken never asked that the ballpark fences be moved in.

– Art Thiel

The gloves come out in left field during batting practice. Fans wondered if an All-Star would become the first to hit a ball out of Safeco Field, but it didn't happen PHOTOGRAPH BY MIKE URBAN

A STAR AMONG STARS

JULY 9 — Willie Randolph intently watched him from outside the batting cage.

It wasn't long before Don Zimmer rushed over to shake his hand.

Alex Rodriguez and Barry Bonds worked their way through the crowd for a greeting.

With the All-Star Game workout serving as a backdrop, Ichiro appeared at Safeco Field the same as he has all season.

The 27-year-old rookie outfielder became an instant hit.

All the while, Ichiro displayed a toothy grin and smooth demeanor, as routine as his at-bats.

"Thank you. It's amazing," Ichiro said when it was time for him to address a throng of admirers after receiving an award for being the top vote-get-ter in All-Star balloting.

Ichiro also became the first rookie to win the overall fan balloting, with 3,373,035 votes.

And Ichiro might have accomplished another first, promptly parking the first three pitches he saw during batting practice into the right-field bleachers. His first four hits were homers.

"He's surprising American baseball, and I'm glad he's here," said Bonds, the National League's leading vote-getter.

Wearing his hat and sunglasses backward for most of the workout, Ichiro seemed unfazed by the attention. He is supposed to be a rookie. He is supposed to be a foreigner, but he owned the place.

"He's exactly what people should be talking about," Rodriguez said. "He'd probably win the Home Run Derby if he entered it."

– Ronald Tillery

Ichiro is the fans' choice. The newcomer from Japan was top vote-getter in fan balloting that determined the lineups and a main attraction during All-Star workouts.

PHOTOGRAPH BY
MERYL SCHENKER

THE SEASON CONTINUED FROM PAGE 62

SEATTLE (JULY 15) – Last Tuesday night, All-Stars such as Cal Ripken and Alex Rodriguez and Barry Bonds were playing at Safeco Field.

Tonight, there was Scott Podsednik, at the same ballpark, creating just as much excitement. In less than a week, baseball in Seattle went from Hall of Fame to no-name.

After clearing the bases with a pinch-hit triple, Podsednik co-starred with the more prominent Aaron Sele in the Mariners' 8-0 victory over Arizona.

Switching places when the Mariners sent pitcher Dennis Stark to Tacoma on July 5, Podsednik had been a seldom-used reserve on Lou Piniella's bench. In the seventh inning tonight, he was summoned to pinch hit.

For the first time as a major leaguer, Podsednik stepped into the batter's box. Arizona reliever Erik Sabel decided to go with his strongest pitch – a sinker. On a 1-and-0 delivery, Sabel threw one that stayed up in the strike zone. Podsednik stroked it to the gap in left-center field and took off.

While John Olerud, Bret Boone and Mike Cameron scored before him, Podsednik was on his horse, flying to third while center fielder Steve Finley fumbled the ball on the warning track.

Podsednik had a shot at an inside-the-park home run, but third-base coach Dave Myers threw up the stop sign. Podsednik scored on David Bell's single as the crowd continued to buzz.

When he went to left field in the top of the eighth, Podsednik was greeted with a standing ovation.

"I had electricity flowing through me," Podsednik said. "With 50,000 people hollering and screaming, I can't describe it. It's something I've been dreaming about since I was a young kid."

– Jim Moore

SEATTLE (JULY 26) – Joel Pineiro isn't sure he will get another start, but after a dazzling performance tonight in a 4-0 victory over Kansas City, manager Lou Piniella sees a long stint in the starting rotation for the rookie right-hander.

"I like his stuff," Piniella said. "He's added a

Shortstop Carlos Guillen tags out the Diamondbacks' Mark Grace. Guillen hit .312 and committed only one error in July. PHOTOGRAPH BY MIKE URBAN

changeup that's a big pitch for him. And he's a competitive kid."

The 22-year-old Pineiro has a fresh arm. He's a pitcher other teams haven't seen much of. And after Pineiro limited Kansas City to one hit in six innings, that's a trump card Piniella is eager to play.

"He gives us a different look," Piniella said. "This is the time of the season where that's important. I was very pleased. Now I'd like to see him follow it up a few more times."

In a season of good performances by the starters, Pineiro turned in one of the best. He retired 18 of the 19 hitters he faced, walking none and striking out six. By that point he had thrown 78 pitches, and it was time to turn the game over to the bullpen.

"Joel was a tough act to follow," reliever Arthur Rhodes said. Rhodes, Jeff Nelson and Kazuhiro Sasaki each pitched an inning of relief, bringing a two-game losing streak to an end. At the 102-game mark of the season, the Mariners still haven't lost three games in succession.

– John Hickey

> "IT'S FRUSTRATING TO PLAY AGAINST THEM, BUT ON THE OTHER HAND, IT'S PRETTY FUN TO WATCH. THEY GO UP THERE AND THEY HAVE A PLAN AND THEY STICK TO IT. WE'RE TRYING TO GET TO WHAT THEY DO."
> **- Twins first baseman Doug Mientkiewicz**

AUGUST
Moyer dominates another 20-win month

NEW YORK (AUG. 17) – Seattle reliever Jeff Nelson was given his fourth World Series ring in a ceremony before tonight's game.

Nelson, with the Yankees as they won four championships in five years, was close to being the most popular player in the Mariners clubhouse after the game.

Teammates, most of whom haven't earned rings, wanted to look at it. Most of them wanted to try it on.

Center fielder Mike Cameron, one of those who took an admiring glance at the ring, said it's a "little reminder of what we're playing for."

Tonight's starting pitcher, Paul Abbott, tried it on, too. Abbott has a ring, the result of $3\frac{1}{2}$ months of work with the 1991 Twins. But he never wears it.

"To me, you earn a ring by what you do in the postseason," Abbott said. "I helped get them there, but I didn't do anything in the postseason. I'm

Jamie Moyer bears down. The veteran left-hander went 5-0 in his first six starts after the All-Star Game.

PHOTOGRAPH BY
GRANT M. HALLER

waiting to get one with these guys."

The presentation to Nelson was made by Yankees manager Joe Torre, with whom Nelson had some harsh words last year. All that was in the past, however, as they hugged near home plate.

The Yankee Stadium crowd was mostly appreciative, and Nelson tipped his cap to the Yankees dugout and then to the Yankees bullpen before saluting the crowd.

"Hopefully, the guys in here will look at this and remember this is why we play every day," Nelson said. "When you first get into baseball, your goal is the major leagues. When you get to the major leagues, your goal is a ring."

– John Hickey

NEW YORK (AUG. 19) – Measuring stick?

Or whuppin' stick?

Doesn't really matter. The Mariners hit with both today.

Entering the weekend match between baseball's best teams in Aught One, the story line was a late-season size-up that could foretell events of the fall.

It started out well Friday for the Yankees with a shutout victory. Even New York's dramatic, wrenching loss Saturday was dismissed as a freak, owing to a poor outing by a rookie pitcher who will not see the playoffs.

But as the hardball festivities concluded today, here was the measure: The Mariners won the

Mark McLemore makes a barehanded stop against Cleveland. PHOTOGRAPH BY PAUL KITAGAKI JR.

14
Martinez hits a three-run homer in the 11th inning to beat Boston 6-3. Sasaki picks up his 37th save.

19
Cameron ties a club record with eight RBIs in a 10-2 romp at Yankee Stadium.

22
The Mariners tie the franchise record with their 91st victory, a 16-1 rout of the Tigers at Safeco Field.

game, 10-2; the series, 2-1; the season series, 6-3; and finished the regular season 5-1 at Yankee Stadium.

Maestro of the whuppin' stick in the series finale was center fielder Mike Cameron, whose two home runs and eight RBIs had the New York writers scrambling to the conclusions about the Ken Griffey Jr. trade that Mariners fans had arrived at long ago.

Coupled with the icy coolness of Jamie Moyer's seven-hit, one-run marvel, the Mariners' image of resourceful resilience remains intact after the biggest seasonal test yet.

If they don't break it in New York, they seem unlikely to break it anywhere.

– Art Thiel

SEATTLE (AUG. 23) – It didn't take long for Ichiro to move back into the American League batting lead.

Ichiro, who entered today's game tied with Cleveland's Roberto Alomar with a .345 average, singled in his first at-bat. And in his second. And again in his fourth. He finished 3-for-4, upping his average to .348.

It's the first time he's been atop the leaderboard since June.

Ichiro's reaction?

"Nothing," he said.

That's just the way hitting coach Gerald Perry likes it.

"I would prefer that any player in his position just not think about it," Perry said. "It's August. We've got five weeks left in the season. All he's got to do now is go about his business like he has been."

Ichiro has a 20-game hitting streak for the second time this season. No player had done that since Juan Gonzalez had two 21-game streaks with the Rangers in 1996.

Ichiro's current streak, which began on Aug. 3, has seen him average .438. He's had three hits in back-to-back games.

"He's not going to stop," Tigers first baseman Tony Clark said. "He's going to get better, possibly. It's scary."

– John Hickey

SEATTLE (AUG. 26) – How many times do the Indians get to undress the Mariners bullpen?

They did it Aug. 5 in Cleveland, coming back from a 12-run deficit to win 15-14, tying the greatest comeback in baseball history.

Today, the Indians undressed Arthur Rhodes, more literally than figuratively, but for the second day in a row, and caught up to the bullpen again, this time 4-3.

Again, Rhodes was asked in front of God, country and all the ships at sea to remove his diamond earrings, making his jewelry more famous than any baubles in the Tower of London.

Robbed of his, ahem, manhood, Rhodes promptly blew the save. A day earlier, he was ejected when he protested the same jewelry infraction.

At this rate, Rhodes' passion for fashion will have the Mariners three games behind Oakland by the end of September.

– Art Thiel

Arthur Rhodes removes his diamond earrings after a complaint by Cleveland batter Omar Vizquel.

PHOTOGRAPH BY
PAUL KITAGAKI JR.

30
With a win against the Devil Rays, the Mariners set a major league record with their 27th consecutive non-losing road series.

SEPTEMBER

5
The Mariners become the second-fastest team in major league history to reach 100 victories.

7
Boone sets an American League record for home runs by a second baseman with 33 and Ichiro sets a major league mark with his 168th single in a 10-1 victory over the Orioles.

SEPTEMBER
The West is won; the rest is history

SEATTLE (SEPT. 3) – It has been the Mariners' mantra all year: "We haven't done anything yet."

While everyone wanted to talk about the World Series lineup in June and assess the team's place in baseball history in July, the Mariners made sure we knew they weren't doing any chicken-counting.

Now, however, they have done something. With their 3-2, 11-inning victory over the Tampa Bay Devil Rays tonight, the Mariners clinched a spot in the postseason. The magic number for the American League West title is seven, but in the unlikely event the Mariners lose all 24 of their remaining games, they would still be the AL wild-card entry. The victory also put Seattle 60 games over .500.

The night also was a celebration of the return of Jay Buhner, who started in left field in his first game at Safeco since last fall.

Buhner, who had surgery on his left foot June 12, clearly wasn't holding back as he slid into the left-field corner chasing a foul ball in the first and got his only hit on an infield single in the fourth.

The slide drew a huge roar from the crowd of 45,728 and made Buhner's first at-bat an even bigger one.

"If there's anybody here who deserves that, it's Jay," Mark McLemore said. "After all he's been through, it's just great to get him back."

– David Andriesen

SEATTLE (SEPT. 9) – Ramon Vazquez got to shake Cal Ripken's hand today.

Ripken has been in the major leagues for 20 years. Vazquez, called up two days ago, has been around for about 20 minutes. But as one former shortstop said goodbye, another said hello. Vazquez made his first big-league start in Ripken's final game in Seattle.

"If I had the chance, I would have told him how much he's meant to baseball, and how big a fan of his I am," Vazquez said. "He's one of the best ever. But there wasn't really time to say

> "I THINK YOU'LL SEE TEAMS TRYING TO DO WHAT THE MARINERS HAVE DONE – PUT PLAYERS ON THE FIELD WHO KNOW THE GAME AND ARE WILLING TO PLAY FOR THE TEAM, AND NOT JUST FOR THEIR STATS."
> - Orioles advance scout Deacon Jones

Carlos Guillen's jersey hangs in the dugout while the Mariners shortstop was being treated for tuberculosis.
PHOTOGRAPH BY DAN DeLONG

anything.

"On Friday, I got my first hit and got to third base, and he congratulated me for that. Today I got to start his last game. That means a whole lot to me. I got to play against Cal Ripken at least once in my career. That's something special."

– John Hickey

19
The Mariners clinch the AL West title and home-field advantage in the playoffs with a 5-0 shutout of the Angels.

OCTOBER

5
The Mariners match the AL record with victory No. 115. Jamie Moyer joins Randy Johnson as the franchise's only 20-game winners.

6
Five pitchers combine for a 1-0 shutout of the Rangers, allowing the Mariners to tie the 1906 Chicago Cubs for the most wins in a season in major league history.

SEPTEMBER 11

REMEMBRANCE
Baseball returns from mourning, wearing the flag

SEPTEMBER 18 — The hours leading up to tonight's game at Safeco Field were filled with the familiar pregame routines, sights and sounds. Ankles were taped. Baseballs were shagged. Pleas for autographs were shouted from behind the dugout. But like the rest of American workplaces, Safeco felt a little different.

4:40 p.m.: The Mariners are sitting in right field, stretching before batting practice. A plane flies over the stadium. Once, nobody would have noticed. This time a few heads tilt to watch it go past.

Suddenly, "God Bless America" booms over the public-address system. The Gospel Outreach Youth Choir of Olympia is practicing, as the anthem singer does before every game, but has two songs on this night rather than one.

The anthem rehearsal would normally go unnoticed, but most of the players turn to watch. A TV news crew tapes the performance. Afterward, there is a smattering of applause, a rare, if not unheard of, event. A Japanese reporter asks in halting English the name of the first song. "Ah, so that is 'God Bless America,'" she says. She has never heard it before.

5:37 p.m.: The Mariners return to the clubhouse after batting practice to find their jerseys hanging in their lockers. Above their names, where the Major League Baseball logo normally sits, there is an American flag patch. Aside from two small sections of the carpet, they are about the only red things in the room, and stand out sharply.

Pitcher Jeff Nelson takes a small American flag, one like those given to fans at the gate, and affixes it to his locker with trainer's tape.

6:55 p.m.: The players are introduced to loud cheers. The two ballgirls are introduced as usual, and they hold a small banner that says, "America, We Stand United." The stands are full, and a dozen flags hang from the railings. Not a single visible sign in the stadium is baseball-related. Even the now-familiar neon-green sign in the outfield, on this night, doesn't say "TWO OUT … SO WHAT." Tonight it says, "IN GOD … WE TRUST."

7 p.m.: The U.S. Marine Corps color guard emerges on the infield. Without cue, fans rise to their feet and wave tiny flags. The sound of Judy Collins singing "Amazing Grace" a cappella plays behind a scoreboard video montage of pastoral American images as the players line up along the first- and third-base lines.

The color guard walks to the outfield and takes its position to loud cheers. The public-address announcer calls for a moment of silence, which is dutifully observed but lasts a mere 20 seconds.

The choir performs "God Bless America" and then "The Star-Spangled Banner." Al Martin, Mark McLemore and Arthur Rhodes listen with heads bowed; the other players face forward solemnly. As the national anthem concludes, a jetliner crosses directly over the stadium. A few thousand hearts skip a beat.

7:09 p.m.: The color guard slowly leaves the field, the players turning to follow its path and not breaking formation until after the flags disappear.

The speakers blare "Starts and Stripes Forever." The Mariners take the field, and at 7:16, Freddy Garcia throws the first pitch to Darin Erstad. It's a ball.

Back to baseball. One small step toward recovery.

— **David Andriesen**

Mark McLemore holds an American flag as the Mariners observe a moment of silence on the pitcher's mound after clinching the AL West Division championship on Sept. 19. PHOTOGRAPH BY PAUL KITAGAKI JR.

Mariners fans show their support during the seventh-inning stretch.

PHOTOGRAPH BY PAUL KITAGAKI JR.

TRUE COLORS

SEPTEMBER 19 – It wasn't the 5-0 victory over the Angels, or the clinching of the American League West title. Both were reasonably expectable. What was unexpected were the postgame moments.

Watching the Mariners find a way to honor achievements, fans and country without histrionics, triteness or bad taste was a seminal moment in a season of greatness, stuck in the heart of a year otherwise from a steamy sub-basement of hell.

During a period in which the region has endured riots, an energy crisis, an earthquake, the loss of Boeing headquarters and now, sharing with the world an assault on humanity, the Mariners must bear a heavy local load.

They have become, through no fault except their own good works, the best thing going.

Unsurprisingly, they are up to the task.

Sportswriters are often guilty of stretching a ball-game too far to make a point about real life, so no sweeping connections will be made between the baseball joyousness here and the recent obscenities. But the human virtues at play are universal.

What can be said, without exaggeration, is that this group cares a good deal about each other and their public. The moments after the clinching game – especially the prayerful gathering upon bended knees, and the acknowledgement of their supporters – were manifestations of the character that has helped make them successful.

Lou Piniella and the players had talked beforehand about what should be done about a division title, but mostly, things happened spontaneously for a team frequently intuitive in many things regarding the right way.

One of the truest hallmarks of professionals in any endeavor is the ability to devote complete concentration to the task at hand, without distraction from the past or the future. If there is one quality that has allowed the Mariners to win every road series, to have no more than a two-game losing streak, and to rebound from every setback, it is the ability to flourish in the moment.

The feat is elusive, mastered by few. The Mariners have many practitioners.

"One of the great things about this team is that nobody has been talking about next year, or their next contract," Jamie Moyer said. "Nobody talks about the postseason, until now. Nobody talks about tomorrow's game. The talk is about today."

In a time when the past is horrific, the future uncertain, the virtue has resonance beyond baseball. And in a time of rampant cynicism about professional athletes, it is a pleasure to offer up the opinion that beyond their baseball skills, these are good people, with a collective sense beyond themselves.

That is not to say other teams are not populated by similar figures. Nor does it mean that the Mariners are without flaw, fault or shortcoming.

It simply means that this is a collection of people who have done their seasonal jobs with uncommon skill, to a level almost unprecedented in a century of baseball, yet managed to focus almost completely on the moment, without losing sight of what matters.

These days, it's a good feeling to experience people who do extraordinary things well.

– Art Thiel

Enjoying the moment, manager Lou Piniella watched his team clinch the AL West title on Sept. 19.

PHOTOGRAPH BY PAUL KITAGAKI JR.

OCTOBER
Matching baseball's best victory total

"WE GAVE IT A GREAT RUN, AND THE FANS HAVE BEEN UNBELIEVABLE. I'VE NEVER SEEN FANS LIKE THE ONES HERE, EVER."
- Bret Boone

With Mike Cameron front and center, the Mariners celebrate their 116th victory, tying a major league record set in 1906 by the Chicago Cubs. The clincher came on the next-to-last day of the season. PHOTOGRAPH BY DAN DeLONG

SEATTLE (OCT. 5) – Most teams with a division title already in their pocket treat the regular season's 160th outing as a throwaway – run half your Class AAA team out there, don't get anybody hurt and let's all go home early. The 2001 Mariners, of course, are not most teams.

There might have been no other game this season the Mariners wanted to win more than tonight's against Texas. They had a chance to claim their 115th victory, breaking a tie with the 1998 Yankees for the most ever by an American League team, and starting pitcher Jamie Moyer was going for his 20th win.

So the Mariners swung for the fences. They crashed into walls. They got their uniforms dirty. And they beat the Rangers, 6-2, before a sellout crowd at Safeco Field.

"We go after it hard, one through nine, every night, and that's what we did tonight," manager Lou Piniella said. "To think that a team could go through the entire season winning seven out of every 10 games they played, to get the AL road record for wins with 59 and now the all-time winning record in the American League, 115. That only comes around once in a lifetime."

After the final out, Piniella met each player in front of the dugout with a hug. He has been in baseball for four decades and had tremendous success, but he's never seen anything quite like this.

"I really can't tell you how proud I am," he said. "It has just been a joy and a pleasure all year to manage this team."

– David Andriesen

THE POSTSEASON

AL DIVISION SERIES
Indians make it tough, but Mariners survive in five

GAME 1:
INDIANS 5, MARINERS 0

	1	2	3	4	5	6	7	8	9	R	H	E
Cleveland	0	0	0	3	0	1	0	1	0	5	11	1
Seattle	0	0	0	0	0	0	0	0	0	0	6	1

BARTOLO COLON HAD the most fun of anyone today. Mariners starter Freddy Garcia, who had a lapse in the fourth inning, had the least.

Cleveland scored three times in the fourth as the first six batters reached base. Juan Gonzalez, Travis Fryman and Marty Cordova had run-scoring hits.

At the end of the inning, the Mariners were down 3-0 en route to giving away the home-field advantage. They brought the tying run to the plate only once, when Ichiro flied out to end the fifth with two men on base. It was the only out Ichiro made, as he had three of Seattle's six hits, including a double.

"Colon was awesome today," Garcia said, casting a covetous view at Colon's statistics – six hits, two walks, no runs. "When he throws like that, he's going to be unhittable."

How unhittable? The 2-3-4-5-6 men in the Mariners order – Mark McLemore, Bret Boone, Edgar Martinez, John Olerud and Mike Cameron – were 1-for-19 against Colon. In the regular season, those hitters combined for 519 RBIs.

– John Hickey

NEXT TIME THE invitation list is made up, don't invite the Cleveland Indians. They spoil a party like unbathed relatives who insist on pan-flute music.

Here Seattle was, all set to have a history-book-burning party, and the Indians show up with fire hoses.

They don't get it. This was supposed to be the Mariners' moment, the Mariners' season. But today the Indians not only won the first game of a five-game series, they dominated it. How rude.

This wasn't supposed to happen, not in front of the biggest crowd ever at the ballyard, at the commencement of postseason festivities.

Indians starter Bartolo Colon made the Mariners look so bad, people were inspecting the number 116 to see if it had a decimal in it.

Colon was so tough – 99-mph tough – that the best way to get around him might just be to not face him until next season.

That would involve winning the next three games. Since the Mariners have done the improbable with great regularity this season, there is no reason to eliminate the possibility.

Still, if Ichiro is the only guy bringing offense, three consecutive victories may have to wait until "B" games next spring in Peoria.

– Art Thiel

Starting pitcher Freddy Garcia feels the pain of a three-run Indians rally in the fourth inning. PHOTOGRAPH BY MIKE URBAN

GAME 2:
MARINERS 5, INDIANS 1

	1	2	3	4	5	6	7	8	9		R	H	E
Cleveland	0	0	0	0	0	0	1	0	0		1	6	0
Seattle	4	0	0	0	1	0	0	0	x		5	5	0

AS SOON AS Mike Cameron's bat connected with Chuck Finley's pitch, it was all over.

Sure, there was still plenty of baseball yet to be played this afternoon. But when the Mariners center fielder swung, when his bat made that special resonating "thunk" that brings fans to their feet, the frustrations of the past two days were gone in an instant.

Cameron's two-run home run, over the hand-operated scoreboard in left field that had displayed so many Mariners zeros two days before, did more than give Seattle a first-inning lead. It breathed life back into Safeco Field and restored the confident optimism that had sustained a city for six months.

The Mariners were back.

Cameron's shot was followed by a Bret Boone

single and a two-run shot over the center-field wall by Edgar Martinez. With 20-game winner Jamie Moyer on the mound for the Mariners, a 4-0 lead just about closed the deal with eight innings to play. Good night, drive safely and don't forget to tip your waitress.

– David Andriesen

JAMIE MOYER, WHO allowed five hits in six-plus innings, left with a 5-0 lead. The Indians' only run scored when Jeff Nelson induced a bases-loaded double play in the seventh.

Not bad for a fellow whose day started just like yours might have. Moyer got up and played chauffeur, driving his kids to school. That got him to Safeco Field just before 8:30 a.m.

"I got here at 8:30, and Jamie was already here," Jay Buhner said. "He was already locked in."

Moyer, a 20-game winner for the first time in his career, has been locked in most of the season. He's won 12 of his past 13 decisions. The one today, he acknowledged, was the biggest yet.

"This is a dream come true," Moyer said after his first postseason victory. "And it was a team effort, and we played well together."

Then it was time for the Locked-In Man and his teammates to catch the bus and head for Sea-Tac and a flight to Cleveland, where Seattle needs to win at least one of two games.

The Mariners won 59 road games this season, a major league record, including three of four in Cleveland.

"I expect that we'll go to Cleveland and have the same results," Moyer said.

– John Hickey

Jamie Moyer extends his mastery into the postseason, frustrating the Indians with offspeed pitches.

PHOTOGRAPH BY PAUL KITAGAKI JR.

Mariners fans go wild as Moyer strikes out Cleveland slugger Jim Thome.

PHOTOGRAPH BY MIKE URBAN

Cleveland catcher Einar Diaz tags out Dan Wilson in the fourth inning as the Mariners slumped to the brink of elimination.

PHOTOGRAPH BY
MIKE URBAN

GAME 3:
INDIANS 17, MARINERS 2

	1	2	3	4	5	6	7	8	9	R	H	E
Seattle	1	0	0	0	0	0	1	0	0	2	7	3
Cleveland	2	2	4	0	1	3	0	5	x	17	19	0

HOW A TEAM that won 116 games can look triple-feeble in its biggest contest of the season will become one of the great questions in the sporting cosmos.

But hey, the Mariners have done nothing but surprise all year.

Why not a swan dive into the slag heap?

To suspect that the Mariners were capable of a 17-2 defeat in the playoffs was to imagine Julia Roberts weighing 400 pounds.

The gentle observation is "go figure;" the accurate observation is "disfigure." Losing a game is one thing; to screw up in a way that would embarrass Elmer Fudd is something else.

They went from flawless in Game 2 to helpless in Game 3. Meanwhile, the suddenly muscular Cleveland Indians appeared to be capable of digging another Great Lake and getting home by lunch.

But here's the good news for Mariners fans. The series count is 1-2, not 0-300, and all the players were accounted for in the clubhouse, providing no evidence that they went though some star-gate time warp with the '81 Mariners.

And there's better news:

"It may have been 17 runs, but it was one game," said Mike Cameron.

A bad game, a horrible game, the worst all season and one of the ghastliest in postseason history, but one game.

– **Art Thiel**

Edgar Martinez smiles after his two-run home run in the ninth gave the Mariners some breathing room.

PHOTOGRAPH BY MIKE URBAN

GAME 4:
MARINERS 6, INDIANS 2

	1	2	3	4	5	6	7	8	9	R	H	E
Seattle	0	0	0	0	0	0	3	1	2	6	11	0
Cleveland	0	1	0	0	0	0	1	0	0	2	5	2

DOWN TO THEIR final nine outs in a game that could have ended their record-setting season, the Mariners came up big, rising from the ashes for a 6-2 victory over Cleveland in Game 4 of the American League Division Series.

Things looked bleak for the Mariners, who were down 1-0 to Indians ace Bartolo Colon after six innings. Colon had shut them out for 14 consecutive innings. While the Indians had only a home run by Juan Gonzalez off Freddy Garcia, that one run made for a gargantuan difference.

The Mariners could feel it.

"After 116 wins, after leading the league in hitting, pitching and defense, we couldn't lose the last game 1-0," reliever Jeff Nelson said. "But we hadn't done anything for six innings. You're thinking, 'Oh, my God….'"

Without the need for divine intervention, the Mariners put on a rally that encapsulated their season. They did it by parlaying a walk, a hit-and-run single and a sacrifice fly into a run that tied the game. It was textbook Mariners baseball.

Having drawn even on David Bell's sacrifice, the Seattle hitters awoke from a semi-coma to score five more times. All of a sudden, their five-hour flight home could be condensed from funereal to fun.

– John Hickey

Lou Piniella argues a call with home plate umpire Rick Reed. Piniella lost the argument, but not the game.
PHOTOGRAPH BY MIKE URBAN

GAME 5:
MARINERS 3, INDIANS 1

	1	2	3	4	5	6	7	8	9	R	H	E
Cleveland	0	0	1	0	0	0	0	0	0	1	4	0
Seattle	0	2	0	0	0	0	1	0	x	3	9	1

IN THE FOURTH inning of an achingly taut 2-1 game, Jamie Moyer struck out the 4-5-6 guts of the Indians lineup: Juan Gonzalez, Ellis Burks and Jim Thome. Looking. And looking helpless.

Never this season had Moyer struck out the side.

And he did it on three days' rest in a must-win postseason game against a playoff-savvy lineup that was second in American League batting average and three days earlier scored 17 runs. The Mariners won the game, 3-1, the series, 3-2, and won over at least some of the skeptics who figured the number 116 was police code for baseball fraud.

Moyer's three whiffs were part of 10 consecutive outs among the final 10 batters he faced. His six innings of one-run, three-hit ball today, following 20 innings of two runs over three games against Cleveland in 2001, was nothing short of astonishing.

"Great pitchers come through at the right time," Indians second baseman Roberto Alomar said. "He came through."

– Art Thiel

Edgar Martinez didn't want to come out of Game 5. So what if he could barely run? His injured groin was the only body part reminding him that he has, indeed, reached his 38th birthday.

Yet the Mariners' designated hitter and longest active player graciously complied, giving way to pinch-runner Al Martin in the eighth inning of Seattle's 3-1, division series-clinching victory over the Cleveland Indians.

He had done his job, sharply singling home an insurance run.

It was just like the day before in Ohio, when he smacked a two-run, 458-foot home run in the ninth inning to cap a 6-2 victory, assuring a Game 5.

And it was similar to three days before that, when he slugged a two-run, first-inning homer, propelling the Mariners to a 5-1 victory in Game 2 at Safeco Field.

If it's not clear already, Martinez won't be leaving this line of work any time soon. They're going to have to carry him out, cleats and bats first.

– Dan Raley

> "WE TOOK THEM TO FIVE GAMES, AND THEY'RE THE BEST TEAM IN BASEBALL. THEY'RE A LITTLE BETTER THAN WE ARE. THEY DIDN'T WIN 116 GAMES BY LUCK."
> **- Indians pitcher Chuck Finley**

At a game where fan frenzy was rewarded, John Logae of Woodinville appeared as an Ichiro bobblehead doll. His hero set a division series record by hitting .600.

PHOTOGRAPH BY
PAUL KITAGAKI JR.

Mike Cameron leaps for joy on his way to the clubhouse. The Mariners had just earned a spot in the American League Championship Series.

PHOTOGRAPH BY MIKE URBAN

CLEVELAND GENERAL MANAGER John Hart headed home tonight, happy to leave Ichiro Suzuki behind.

"What he did to us in the playoffs, he shouldn't have done," Hart said. "I mean, that's unfair."

What Ichiro did to the Indians was hit against them when his teammates couldn't. The Mariners hit .247 in the five-game series, but if you throw out Ichiro's numbers, they hit .196 – 92 points below their regular-season batting average.

The rookie right fielder from Japan hit .600 against the Indians – a record for a five-game American League Division Series, and a career ALDS record for anyone with at least 20 at-bats.

He scored a quarter of the Mariners' runs in the series, and had 31 percent of their hits. His slug-ging percentage was .650, even though he had just one extra-base hit, a double in Game 1. He led off all five games by reaching base, three times on singles, once on a walk and once on an error.

There were eight innings in the series in which the Mariners scored. Five of them featured a hit by Ichiro, another an Ichiro walk.

While his teammates flailed against Bartolo Colon and the rest of Cleveland's power pitchers, all Ichiro did was better his regular-season batting average by 250 points.

Without Ichiro, the Mariners would not be play-ing anymore. They know it, and they fully appreci-ate their good fortune.

– David Andriesen

AL CHAMPIONSHIP SERIES
The joy ride ends in New York, stopped by a dynasty

GAME 1:
YANKEES 4, MARINERS 2

	1	2	3	4	5	6	7	8	9	R	H	E
New York	0	1	0	2	0	0	0	0	1	4	9	0
Seattle	0	0	0	0	1	0	0	0	1	2	4	0

THE MARINERS DEPLOYED on the mound today their own high-priced free agent, Aaron Sele, who performed decently enough – three runs in six innings – and certainly better than his previous start against Cleveland.

But he wasn't Mr. Doorslam. He offered up a Chuck Finley inning – a leadoff double to Jorge Posada, followed by a home run to Paul O'Neill – in the fourth that is typically all the Yankees need this time of year.

If the Mariners can't get a lead, they can't deploy their big weapon, the bullpen. And today, Andy Pettitte threw a no-hitter for four innings, then quieted a good-looking rally in the fifth by getting John Olerud to ground out, and striking out Jay Buhner and Dan Wilson.

After that, a quiet of cathedral proportions fell upon the Mariners lineup.

– Art Thiel

THE MARINERS DIDN'T win today. Didn't really come close to beating the Yankees in Game 1 of the American League Championship Series. Yet there was a victory within the setback.

Carlos Guillen played.

At Safeco Field, on a crisp October afternoon, he took a deep breath and reclaimed his shortstop position.

Breathing is good after you have contracted tuberculosis.

Nineteen days and 14 missed games after a shocking diagnosis, Guillen was back in the Seattle lineup, batting second, gloving every ball sent his way and even ranging into center field for one that wasn't.

The native of Maracay, Venezuela, got a nice round of applause once he took the field, a standing ovation for his first at-bat and a respectful fist bump from New York's Chuck Knoblauch while covering second base.

"I was really excited," Guillen said softly, a little overwhelmed by the crush of reporters backing him up. "It's been a couple of weeks. I didn't think I could come back and play this year."

He still doesn't know how he contracted the disease, nor where. He lost 12 pounds, and gained all but two of them back. He's on medication for the next six months.

As expected, Guillen looked a little rusty swinging a bat. He went 0-for-3 against Yankees lefty Andy Pettitte, grounding out, flying out and striking out, before giving way to pinch-hitter Stan Javier in the ninth.

Guillen gave a wave to the fans when they acknowledged his first appearance at short.

For his first at-bat, the ovation was louder, Guillen hesitating briefly before stepping in against Pettitte.

"It was nice to see him out there," second baseman Bret Boone said. "The fans gave him a nice ovation. He deserved that, after what he's been through."

– Dan Raley

Chuck Knoblauch slides safely into second, ahead of Bret Boone's tag.

Reliever Jose Paniagua shows the strain of pitching in the ninth.

PHOTOGRAPHS BY PAUL KITAGAKI JR.

Bret Boone tosses his bat after flying out to center field, as the Mariners offense continued to struggle.

PHOTOGRAPH BY
PAUL KITAGAKI JR.

GAME 2:
YANKEES 3, MARINERS 2

	1	2	3	4	5	6	7	8	9		R	H	E
New York	0	3	0	0	0	0	0	0	0		3	9	1
Seattle	0	0	0	2	0	0	0	0	0		2	6	0

THE YANKEES' DIVISION-series comeback against Oakland started with great pitching and timely hitting. The Mariners will need those commodities in XXL sizes to get the job done. The Mariners are 0-for-10 in the first two games of the championship series with men in scoring position after going 0-for-6 tonight.

Seattle got one huge hit, a two-run homer by Stan Javier in the fourth after the Yankees had jumped out to a 3-0 lead.

But time and again against starter Mike Mussina and relievers Ramiro Mendoza and Mariano Rivera, Mariners hitters couldn't deliver. Seattle left men in scoring position in the first, second and third innings against Mussina, and again in the seventh against Mendoza.

For all their opportunities with men at second or third, the Mariners got nothing. Which is why they boarded their charter for New York tonight without a win in the series.

– John Hickey

MAYBE LOU PINIELLA had Game 6 of the 2000 American League Championship Series on his mind tonight when he erupted the way only Lou Piniella can.

Maybe the Mariners manager was thinking about when his team ran out of steam last October, when it challenged the reigning World Series champions through six games of the ALCS and felt that in time – and with a deeper bullpen – the Mariners might have a good shot at toppling the dynasty.

Apparently, despite the non-performance of his hitters so far this postseason, Piniella still thinks now is the time.

The Yankee mystique?

"There's no mystique," Piniella said.

Unbeatable?

"They can be beaten."

Sweet Lou? Oh, no. That was Red-Hot Lou tonight. A former Yankee who apparently is sick and tired of the people in pinstripes.

There isn't any other way to describe Piniella as he stormed into the interview room at Safeco Field after his team dropped into an 0-2 hole against the Yankees and issued a declaration heard 'round the world.

"I want you all to print this," Piniella said. "We're coming back here for Game 6."

– Laura Vecsey

GAME 3:
MARINERS 14, YANKEES 3

	1	2	3	4	5	6	7	8	9	R	H	E
Seattle	0	0	0	2	7	2	1	2		14	15	0
New York	2	0	0	0	0	0	0	1	0	3	7	2

IF LOU PINIELLA pulls off this comeback, he gets elected mayor of Seattle AND New York.

After being mocked in the tabloids for forecasting a return of the American League Championship Series to Seattle for Game 6, Piniella had a rare team meeting before Game 3 today. Instructions were given on the heretofore hidden art of, as the Mariners manager put it so vividly the other day, kicking Yankee asses.

As Edgar Martinez recalled:

"He just said to play hard and have fun."

Jeez. Who woulda thought?

By a count of 14-3, pinstriped backsides were indeed indented.

Or, to put it in New York Post headline style: Mystique this.

Baseball's Nostradamus is halfway home.

Whether Piniella's promise, or his meeting, had direct impact on today's glacial outburst will remain unknown, since baseball can't quantify it with a statistic. Certainly, it gave the city and national baseball media something to buzz about, perhaps keeping them from picking apart the tepid Mariners offense.

What is more documentable is that the postseason legend Orlando Hernandez wasn't his usual playoff self. Neither was the entire Yankees lineup, at bat or in the field.

But this time, the Mariners finally exploited the New York ordinariness, with an ALCS record for runs in one game. Their whopper sixth inning of seven runs was the most in a playoff game against the Yankees since 1958.

– Art Thiel

Left fielder Stan Javier leaps high to take a home run away from Alfonso Soriano in the third inning, keeping the game within reach.

PHOTOGRAPH BY MIKE URBAN

GAME 4:
YANKEES 3, MARINERS 1

	1	2	3	4	5	6	7	8	9	R	H	E
Seattle	0	0	0	0	0	0	0	1	0	1	2	0
New York	0	0	0	0	0	0	0	1	2	3	4	0

BEFORE THEY ERECT a statue of a rookie second baseman, the Yankees might want to construct one of Arthur Rhodes, the man they love to see on the mound in a tight moment.

It's difficult to blame Rhodes completely for one of the most agonizing losses in Mariners history. The offense, after a one-game anomaly in Game 3, resumed its postseason snooze against a beatable Roger Clemens. And Kazuhiro Sasaki, absent from the postgame interviews, was the pitcher who gave up a preposterous game-winning homer to Alfonso Soriano, a rookie batting ninth.

But when baseball historians a hundred years from now examine the archives, they will see that bad things happened when Rhodes and the Yanks got together in the little Seattle-New York rivalry of Aught-Aught and Aught-One.

Tonight, in a freakishly entertaining Game 4, Rhodes in the eighth inning went macho on the Yankees' cleanup hitter, Bernie Williams, trying to bust him in with a fastball.

Williams hit what Rhodes swore was a pop-up.

But the parabola arced deeper and deeper. When it landed four rows into the intimate right-field grandstand of breezy Yankee Stadium, it set up a plunge into a hole darker than the Mariners have experienced this season.

They lost 3-1 and are down 3-1 to the champs entering the fifth game tomorrow, which offers up the Yankees' second-favorite Mariners pitcher, starter Aaron Sele. They may snooze on a Bronx bench, so eager are they to get to the park for their hacks.

"Well, this puts us in a rather precarious position," said Lou Piniella, still holding to a light game face. "Outside of that, we gave it the best we could. It was a great ballgame. We didn't lose; we just got beat."

– Art Thiel

Game 4 was a mixed bag in every way, throughout the game, for both teams. It was a thrilling, strange game whose outcome wouldn't be known until the final pitch was thrown.

Perhaps no part of it was stranger than the line of Mariners starter Paul Abbott: 5 innings, 0 hits, 0 runs, 8 walks. Nobody could remember ever seeing anything like it.

Abbott retired the Yankees in order in the first inning, then walked two men in each of the next four innings, throwing 97 pitches – only 49 for strikes – before giving way to Norm Charlton to start the sixth. Abbott fell one shy of the LCS record for walks in a game – and they came in only four innings.

The Yankees, however, couldn't capitalize. They never even got a runner to third base against Abbott. In the second inning, both baserunners were caught stealing. In the third, fourth and fifth, the Yankees went down with runners on first and second. Abbott wasn't quite sure where the ball was going, but the Yankees couldn't hit it.

– David Andriesen

Bret Boone reacts to the "safe" call as New York's Alfonso Soriano steals second base.

PHOTOGRAPH BY
PAUL KITAGAKI JR.

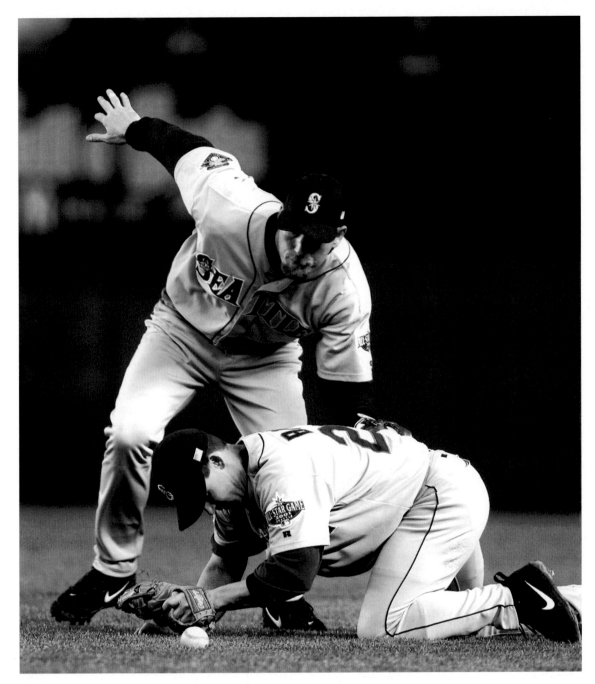

Jay Buhner and Bret Boone fail to catch a ball hit by Chuck Knoblauch, keeping alive a Yankees rally.

PHOTOGRAPH BY DAN DeLONG

GAME 5:
YANKEES 12, MARINERS 3

	1	2	3	4	5	6	7	8	9	R	H	E
Seattle	0	0	0	0	0	0	3	0	0	3	9	1
New York	0	0	4	1	0	4	0	3	x	12	13	1

FOR THE MARINERS, there will be no Fall Classic. Theirs was a classic fall.

Squandering their best chance yet to give Seattle its first World Series, the Mariners completed a American League Championship Series meltdown with a 12-3 loss tonight at Yankee Stadium.

As a result, the Mariners' record-setting regular season — when they won 116 games and led the league in batting average, earned-run average and fielding percentage — becomes a footnote to another chapter in baseball history being written by the Yankees.

"You don't play to set records," shortstop Mark McLemore said. "You play to win the World Series. When you don't, it's very disappointing."

The Mariners led the major leagues in runs scored during the regular season. But against the Yankees, Seattle showed none of that. The Mariners, bogged down by a team batting average of .211, totaled just eight runs in their four losses.

"It wasn't supposed to be like this," Bret Boone said. "It wasn't supposed to end here."

– John Hickey

"GREAT TEAMS DO WHAT THE YANKEES DID."
- Bret Boone

HISTORY WILL NOT be kind to the Mariners, just like the New York Yankees were not kind to the Mariners. In fact, the Yankees were brutal.

Lou Piniella's guarantee of returning to Seattle for Game 6 turned into nothing short of a nightmare tonight. What a quick undoing. What a resounding end to a glorious season – a 12-3 shellacking in Game 5.

Aaron Sele fell to 0-5 against the Yankees in the postseason. Jay Buhner started in right field for the fist time this season, displacing Ichiro and giving Piniella and the Mariners the appearance of a desperate team.

Instant karma did not come for Buhner or the Mariners – not the way Buhner and Bret Boone bungled Chuck Knoblauch's fly ball in the bottom of the sixth, when the Yankees tacked on four more runs.

"It happens. Things snowball. Bloop hits. Home runs. A couple of walks. Whatever bad that could happen happened, but they earned it," center fielder Mike Cameron said after the shocking defeat.

Cruel as it may be, history will be bent on reducing the Mariners to a footnote. Or worse, it will twist the Mariners' 116-win season into the answer to a sports-bar trivia question:

Which team matched the major league record for wins in a season, then lost the ALCS in five games?

It won't help that the Mariners are the team from the farthest reaches of America. They are so easy to dismiss anyway. They are a Pacific time zone castaway unable to consistently crack prime-time consciousness.

History will laud the Yankees for their continued postseason dominance. History will embellish this latest victorious chapter with the way New York has needed and used these Yankees for an important form of communion and catharsis.

For the Mariners, though, history will not be kind – unless there is another version of history; unless there is a version that says you can't take away all those summer nights at Safeco Field.

You can't deny what happened between April 2 and Oct. 7.

You can't take away the awe.

You can't take away the joy.

You can't take away the pleasure of watching the Mariners perform fascinating baseball theater for 162 games.

You can't take away the sellouts and the record-breaking attendance – more than 3.5 million people attended games at Safeco.

You can't take away the magic of Ichiro's rookie season.

You can't take away Edgar Martinez becoming the Mariner who stayed to assume his rightful place as franchise king.

You can't take away Bret Boone's record year for AL second basemen.

You can't take away Jamie Moyer's 20 wins.

You can't take away the chemistry.

You can't take away the satisfaction of a city that spent three seasons watching future Hall of Famers Randy Johnson, Ken Griffey Jr. and Alex Rodriguez seek their fortunes and happiness elsewhere, only to open its eyes to a Mariners team that was better than ever.

There is all of that. Then there is this issue of no World Series appearance, let alone a World Series victory. It's hard to figure that history will not tip the scales against kindness toward the Mariners.

"I think 116 wins will stand for a long time. It's a remarkable season," Mariners president Chuck Armstrong said.

"We brought a lot of excitement, a lot of energy. We played the game right," Buhner said.

"There are always going to be skeptics, and people have a right to say what they want," Boone said.

"This is a little bittersweet, but I don't expect a backlash. I think the fans back home are proud of what we did."

That hometown pride will have to carry the weight of history for the 116-win Mariners.

If that's all the kindness they get, it will be enough. The ones who were there all summer know.

– Laura Vecsey

Carlos Guillen hangs his head in the dugout at Yankee Stadium. The Mariners' record run was over, their best season history. PHOTOGRAPH BY MIKE URBAN

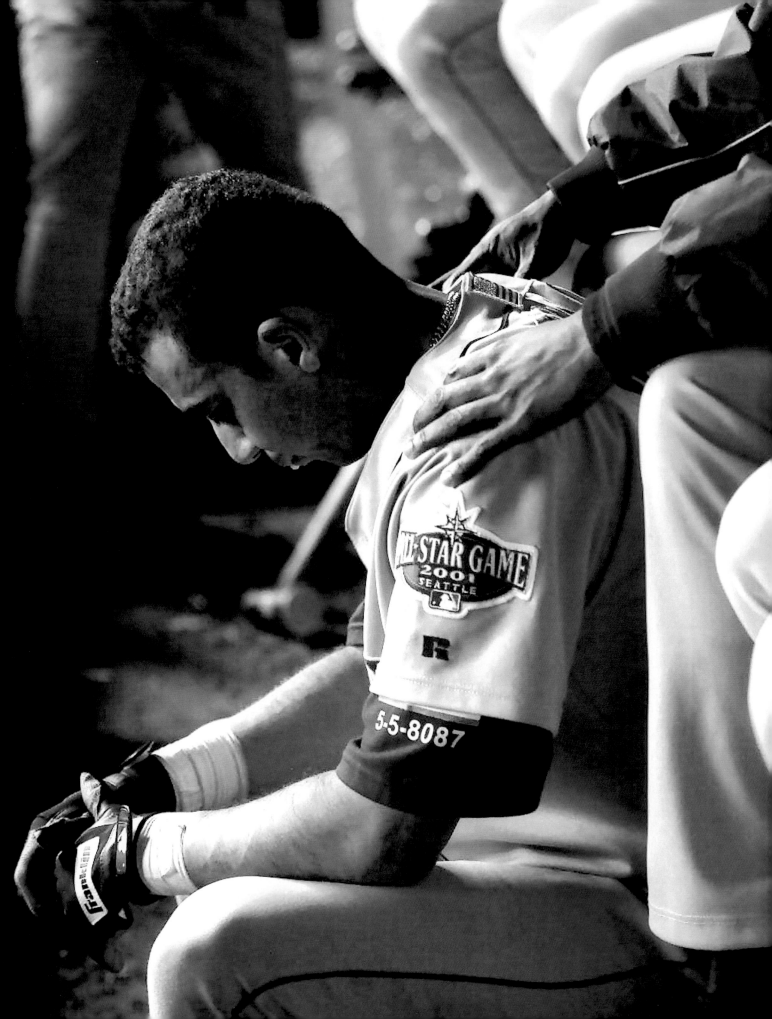

■ WINS ■ LOSSES

APRIL 20-5

MAY 20-7

JUNE 18-9

JULY 18-9

AUGUST 20-9

SEPTEMBER 15-6

OCTOBER 5-1/4-6

APRIL

2 SEA 5, OAK 4
3 OAK 5, SEA 1
4 SEA 10, OAK 2
6 SEA 9, @TEX 7 •
7 SEA 6, @TEX 5
8 @TEX 5, SEA 4
10 SEA 5, @OAK 1
11 SEA 3, @OAK 0
12 SEA 7, @OAK 3
13 @ANA 4, SEA 3
14 SEA 2, @ANA 1
15 SEA 7, @ANA 5
16 SEA 9, TEX 7
17 SEA 6, TEX 4
18 TEX 8, SEA 6
19 SEA 3, ANA 2
20 SEA 4, ANA 1
21 SEA 5, ANA 2
22 SEA 5, ANA 0
24 SEA 7, @NYY 5
25 SEA 7, @NYY 5
26 SEA 7, @NYY 3
27 SEA 8, @CHW 3
28 SEA 8, @CHW 5
29 @CHW 2, SEA 1 •

MAY

1 BOS 2, SEA 0
2 SEA 5, BOS 1
3 SEA 10, BOS 3
4 TOR 8, SEA 3
5 SEA 7, TOR 5
6 TOR 11, SEA 3
8 @BOS 12, SEA 4
9 SEA 10, @BOS 5
10 SEA 5, @BOS 2
11 SEA 7, @TOR 2
12 SEA 11, @TOR 7
13 SEA 7, @TOR 5
15 SEA 4, CHW 3
16 SEA 7, CHW 2
17 SEA 5, CHW 1
18 NYY 14, SEA 10
19 NYY 2, SEA 1 •
20 SEA 6, NYY 2
22 @MIN 12, SEA 11
23 SEA 5, @MIN 4
25 SEA 9, @KC 6
26 SEA 7, @KC 2
27 SEA 5, @KC 4 •

28 SEA 13, @KC 3
29 SEA 3, BAL 2
30 SEA 12, BAL 5
31 SEA 2, BAL 1

JUNE

1 SEA 8, TAM 4
2 SEA 7, TAM 4
3 SEA 8, TAM 4
4 SEA 11, TEX 6
5 SEA 5, TEX 4
6 SEA 7, TEX 3
8 SEA 7, SD 1
9 SD 6, SEA 3
10 SEA 8, SD 1
12 SEA 10, @COL 9
14 @COL 8, SEA 2, 1st
14 SEA 5, @COL 1, 2nd
15 SEA 8, @SD 4
16 SEA 9, @SD 2
17 @SD 11, SEA 9
18 @OAK 4, SEA 3
19 SEA 8, @OAK 7
20 @OAK 6, SEA 4
21 SEA 12, @OAK 10
22 ANA 8, SEA 1
23 ANA 2, SEA 1
24 SEA 7, ANA 3
26 SEA 7, OAK 3
27 OAK 6, SEA 3
28 OAK 6, SEA 3
29 SEA 9, @ANA 5
30 SEA 5, @ANA 3

JULY

1 SEA 5, @ANA 0
2 SEA 9, @TEX 7 •
3 SEA 8, @TEX 4
4 @TEX 6, SEA 3
5 @TEX 14, SEA 2
6 SEA 13, @LA 0
7 @LA 2, SEA 1
8 SEA 9, @LA 2

**July 10
ALL-STAR GAME
AL 4, NL 1
At Safeco Field**

12 SEA 4, SF 3 •
13 SF 5, SEA 3
14 SEA 3, SF 2

15 SEA 8, ARI 0
16 ARI 5, SEA 3
17 SEA 6, ARI 1
18 SEA 2, @KC 0 •
19 @KC 6, SEA 3
20 SEA 4, @MIN 0
21 SEA 6, @MIN 3
22 SEA 6, @MIN 3
23 SEA 3, @MIN 2
24 KC 6, SEA 1
25 KC 5, SEA 1
26 SEA 4, KC 0
27 SEA 11, MIN 4
28 SEA 5, MIN 1
29 SEA 10, MIN 2
31 @DET 4, SEA 2

AUGUST

1 SEA 7, @DET 1
2 SEA 2, @DET 1
3 SEA 2, @CLE 1
4 SEA 8, @CLE 5
5 @CLE 15, SEA 14 •
6 SEA 8, @CLE 6
7 SEA 5, TOR 4 •
8 SEA 12, TOR 4
9 TOR 6, SEA 5
10 CHW 8, SEA 6
11 SEA 4, CHW 3
12 SEA 2, CHW 1
14 SEA 6, @BOS 3 •
15 SEA 6, @BOS 2
16 @BOS 6, SEA 4
17 @NYY 4, SEA 0
18 SEA 7, @NYY 6
19 SEA 10, @NYY 2
20 DET 4, SEA 1
21 SEA 4, DET 1
22 SEA 16, DET 1
23 SEA 5, DET 1
24 SEA 4, CLE 1
25 SEA 3, CLE 2 •
26 CLE 4, SEA 3
28 @TAM 6, SEA 0
29 SEA 5, @TAM 2
30 SEA 4, @TAM 0
31 @BAL 3, SEA 0

SEPTEMBER

1 SEA 6, @BAL 4
2 SEA 1, @BAL 0

3 SEA 3, TAM 2 •
4 TAM 8, SEA 3 •
5 SEA 12, TAM 6
7 SEA 10, BAL 1
8 SEA 6, BAL 1
9 SEA 6, BAL 0
10 SEA 5, @ANA 1

**6 GAMES
POSTPONED BY
TERRORIST
ATTACKS**

18 SEA 4, ANA 0
19 SEA 5, ANA 0
20 ANA 6, SEA 3
21 @OAK 5, SEA 1
22 @OAK 11, SEA 2
23 @OAK 7, SEA 4
24 SEA 9, @TEX 3
25 SEA 13, @TEX 2
26 SEA 7, @TEX 5
28 SEA 5, OAK 3
29 OAK 8, SEA 4
30 SEA 6, OAK 3

OCTOBER

2 SEA 14, @ANA 5
3 SEA 4, @ANA 3
4 SEA 16, TEX 1
5 SEA 6, TEX 2
6 SEA 1, TEX 0
7 TEX 4, SEA 3

ALDS

9 CLE 5, SEA 0
11 SEA 5, CLE 1
13 @CLE 17, SEA 2
14 SEA 6, @CLE 2
15 SEA 3, CLE 1

ALCS

17 NYY 4, SEA 2
18 NYY 3, SEA 2
20 SEA 14, @NYY 3
21 @NYY 3, SEA 1
22 @NYY 12, SEA 3

• Extra-inning game

REGULAR-SEASON HITTING

	AB	R	H	2B	3B	HR	RBI	AVG
Pat Borders	6	1	3	0	0	0	0	.500
Ichiro Suzuki*	692	127	242	34	8	8	69	.350
Eugene Kingsale#	15	4	5	0	0	0	1	.333
Bret Boone	623	118	206	37	3	37	141	.331
Edgar Martinez	470	80	144	40	1	23	116	.306
John Olerud*	572	91	173	32	1	21	95	.302
Ed Sprague	94	9	28	7	0	2	16	.298
Stan Javier#	281	44	82	14	1	4	33	.292
Mark McLemore#	409	78	117	16	9	5	57	.286
Mike Cameron	540	99	144	30	5	25	110	.267
Dan Wilson	377	44	100	20	1	10	42	.265
David Bell	470	62	122	28	0	15	64	.260
Carlos Guillen#	456	72	118	21	4	5	53	.259
Al Martin*	283	41	68	15	2	7	42	.240
Ramon Vazquez*	35	5	8	0	0	0	4	.229
Tom Lampkin*	204	28	46	10	0	5	22	.225
Jay Buhner	45	4	10	2	0	2	5	.222
Charles Gipson	64	16	14	2	2	0	5	.219
Anthony Sanders	17	1	3	2	0	0	2	.176
Scott Podsednik	6	1	1	0	1	0	3	.167
Pitchers	21	2	3	0	0	0	1	.143
Totals	5,680	927	1,637	310	38	169	881	.288

Stolen bases: 174 - Ichiro 56, McLemore 39, Cameron 34, Javier 11, Martin 9, Boone 5, Guillen 4, Martinez 4, Olerud 3, Wilson 3, Kingsale 2, Bell 1, Gipson 1, Javier 1, Lampkin 1

POSTSEASON HITTING

	AB	R	H	2B	3B	HR	RBI	AVG
Ichiro	38	7	16	2	0	0	3	.421
Bell	32	3	8	1	0	1	6	.250
Guillen	8	1	2	0	0	0	0	.250
Martin	4	2	1	0	1	0	0	.250
Javier	22	4	5	1	0	1	2	.227
Martinez	36	4	8	2	0	2	5	.222
Buhner	9	2	2	0	0	1	1	.222
Cameron	35	5	7	5	0	1	3	.200
Boone	40	3	8	0	0	2	6	.200
Olerud	36	3	7	0	0	1	4	.194
Wilson	28	2	5	1	0	0	0	.179
Lampkin	6	0	1	0	0	0	0	.167
McLemore	32	1	5	0	1	0	6	.156
Sprague	1	0	0	0	0	0	0	.000
Gipson	2	1	0	0	0	0	0	.000
Vazquez	0	0	0	0	0	0	0	.000
Totals	329	38	75	12	2	9	36	.228

Stolen bases: 6 - Ichiro 3, Boone, Javier, Martinez

REGULAR-SEASON PITCHING

	W-L	IP	H	R	ER	BB	SO	ERA
Arthur Rhodes*	8-0	68.0	46	14	13	12	83	1.72
Joel Pineiro	6-2	75.1	50	24	17	21	56	2.03
Jeff Nelson	4-3	65.1	30	21	20	44	88	2.76
Norm Charlton*	4-2	47.2	36	19	16	11	48	3.02
Freddy Garcia	18-6	238.2	199	88	81	69	163	3.05
Kazuhiro Sasaki	0-4	66.2	48	24	24	11	62	3.24
Jamie Moyer*	20-6	209.2	187	84	80	44	119	3.43
Ryan Franklin	5-1	78.1	76	32	31	24	60	3.56
Aaron Sele	15-5	215.0	216	93	86	51	114	3.60
Paul Abbott	17-4	163.0	145	79	77	87	118	4.25
Jose Paniagua	4-3	66.0	59	35	32	38	46	4.36
Brian Fuentes*	1-1	11.2	6	6	6	8	10	4.63
John Halama*	10-7	110.1	132	69	58	26	50	4.73
Brett Tomko	3-1	34.2	42	24	20	15	22	5.19
Dennis Stark	1-1	14.2	21	15	15	4	12	9.20
Totals	116-46	1,465	1,293	627	576	465	1,051	3.54

Saves: 56 - Sasaki 45, Nelson 4, Paniagua 3, Rhodes 3, Charlton 1

POSTSEASON PITCHING

	W-L	IP	H	R	ER	BB	SO	ERA
Nelson	0-0	5.1	2	0	0	2	8	0.00
Charlton	0-0	3.1	1	0	0	2	4	0.00
Moyer	3-0	19.0	12	4	4	3	15	1.89
Rhodes	0-0	4.2	3	1	1	0	3	1.93
Garcia	1-2	19.0	20	9	8	7	19	3.79
Sele	0-3	12.0	16	12	6	4	5	4.50
Pineiro	0-0	2.0	4	1	1	2	5	4.50
Halama	0-0	5.0	6	3	3	0	3	5.40
Sasaki	0-1	3.1	3	2	2	0	5	5.40
Abbott	0-0	8.0	9	8	8	13	5	9.00
Paniagua	0-0	5.2	11	11	11	3	2	17.47
Totals	4-6	87.1	87	51	44	36	74	4.53

Saves: 1 - Sasaki

MAJOR LEAGUE
TEAM RECORDS

Victories: 116 (tied)

Games won in April: 20

Games spent in first place: 162 (tied)

Consecutive road series won or tied:
29 (last five of 2000, first 24 of 2001)

MAJOR LEAGUE
INDIVIDUAL RECORDS

Hits by a rookie: 242, Ichiro Suzuki

Games hit safely:
135, Ichiro Suzuki (tied)

Saves in April: 13, Kazuhiro Sasaki

AMERICAN LEAGUE
TEAM RECORDS

Victories: 116

Road victories: 59

AMERICAN LEAGUE
INDIVIDUAL RECORDS

Singles: 192, Ichiro Suzuki

Home runs by a second baseman:
36, Bret Boone

**RBIs by a second baseman (at least
100 games at 2B):** 141, Bret Boone

At-bats by a rookie:
692, Ichiro Suzuki

MARINERS
TEAM RECORDS

Consecutive games won: 15

Victories, homestand: 11

Home victories: 57

Home winning streak: 11

Road winning streak: 7

Most series swept: 16

Fewest series been swept: 1

Players selected to All-Star Game: 8

Home attendance: 3,507,507

Sellouts: 59

Games over .500:
71, 116-45 on October 6

Stolen bases, game:
5 (tied, three times)

Batting average: .287

At-bats: 5,680

**Most players batting .300 or better
(minimum 50 games):** 4 (tied)

Most players, 100 or more hits: 9

Most players, 200 or more hits: 2

Most hits: 1,637

Most singles: 1,120

Most sacrifice flies: 70

Most stolen bases: 174 (tied)

Highest stolen-base percentage: .808

Most runs in a game, both teams:
29 (tied)

Most runs, season, against one club:
140 vs. Texas (20 games)

Most runs, extra-inning game:
14 (vs. Cleveland, 11 innings)

Most runs allowed, extra-inning game:
15 (by Cleveland, 11 innings)

Most runners left on base: 1,257

Lowest earned-run average: 3.54

Most shutouts: 14

Most saves: 56

Fewest hits allowed: 1,293

Fewest runs allowed: 627

Fewest earned runs: 576

Fewest walks issued: 465

**Best winning percentage in one-run
games:** .684

Most victories against one team:
15 vs. Texas and Anaheim

Winning streak against one team:
10 vs. Baltimore (tied)

Fewest players used, season: 32

Highest fielding percentage: .986

Fewest errors: 83

Fewest double plays: 115

Fewest assists: 1,535

MARINERS
INDIVIDUAL RECORDS

At-bats: 692, Ichiro Suzuki

Hits: 242, Ichiro Suzuki

Hits in a game: 5, David Bell (tied)

Sacrifice flies:
13, Bret Boone and Mike Cameron

**Fewest times grounded into double
play (minimum 100 games):**
2, Al Martin (tied)

Hits, career: 1,882, Edgar Martinez

RBIs in a game: 8, Mike Cameron (tied)

Stolen bases in a game:
4, Mark McLemore (tied)

Saves: 45, Kazuhiro Sasaki

Multi-hit games: 75, Ichiro Suzuki

Pitching victories:
20, Jamie Moyer (tied)

Pitching victories, right-hander:
18, Freddy Garcia (tied)

Pitching victories to start a season:
8, Arthur Rhodes (tied)

Saves in a month: 13, Kazuhiro Sasaki

Most consecutive wins:
10, Paul Abbott and Jamie Moyer

Batting average, rookie:
.350, Ichiro Suzuki

Runs, rookie: 127, Ichiro Suzuki

Total bases, rookie: 318, Ichiro Suzuki

Doubles, rookie: 34, Ichiro Suzuki (tied)

Triples, rookie: 8, Ichiro Suzuki (tied)

Stolen bases, rookie: 56, Ichiro Suzuki

Hitting streak, rookie:
23, Ichiro Suzuki

Fielding percentage, catcher:
.999, Dan Wilson

Fielding percentage, outfielder:
.997, Ichiro Suzuki (tied)

AMERICAN LEAGUE
DIVISION SERIES
RECORDS

Highest batting average:
.600, Ichiro Suzuki

Most hits, five-game series:
12, Ichiro Suzuki
(tied Edgar Martinez, 1995)

AMERICAN LEAGUE
CHAMPIONSHIP SERIES
RECORDS

Most runs, game: 14, Game 3

Most hits, inning:
7 (tied), Game 3, 6th inning

Most triples, game:
2 (tied), Mark McLemore,
Al Martin, Game 3

Most RBIs, game:
5 (tied), Bret Boone, Game 3